Women
who Dare
to
Believe

mothers, sisters, daughters of God

VOLUME ONE

by Nan Gurley and Bonnie Keen

with grateful hearts this study is dedicated to
our mothers: *Bernie and Gwen*
our sisters: *Alene, Amy, Kay and Margie*
and our daughters: *Courtney, Erin, and Lena*

Published by New Earth Players Press
copyright 2010 - Nan Gurley and Bonnie Keen

ISBN 0-9776237-2-6
ISBN 978-0-9776237-2-3

Photography and cover art: Ben Arrowood

Book Design: Ben Arrowood and Casey Fay

Edited by Fiona Soltes

Production manager: Wayne Gurley

To order additional copes of this resource, or information about the accompanying musical of the same name, email at www.christianmusicalsforwomen.com.

Printed in the United States of America

TABLE OF CONTENTS

ENDORSEMENTS...PAGE 4

WELCOME ....PAGE 6

THANK YOU ....PAGE 7

MIDWIVES OF EGYPT ....PAGE 8

JOCHEBED ....PAGE 16

MIRIAM ....PAGE 26

PRINCESS OF EGYPT ....PAGE 34

RAHAB...PAGE 40

TAMAR, WIFE OF JUDAH ....PAGE 54

TAMAR, DAUGHTER OF DAVID....................PAGE 64

LEAH...PAGE 76

RACHEL...PAGE 94

ESTHER (PART ONE)....................................PAGE 114

ESTHER (PART TWO) ....PAGE 128

DEBORAH ....PAGE 142

EPILOGUE...PAGE 163

LEADERS GUIDE AND STUDY QUESTIONS ....PAGE 164

ENDNOTES ....PAGE 181

"The Women Who Dare To Believe small group study brings the stories of biblical women to life and the application questions powerfully apply to contemporary issues. This study challenges women to take action steps that produce positive change based on the truth of God's Word. It's refreshingly different from other studies--and it will capture the hearts of your group!"

Carol Kent
www. CarolKent. org
www. SpeakUpSpeakerServices. com
wwwSpeakUpforHope. org

"It never occurred to me that these women of Scripture—who I'd passed over with very little thought—had so much to teach me. What an exciting study! These vividly etched characters—these flesh and blood women of God—provide an astounding vision of the Heavenly Father at work then and now, and helped me connect the dots all the way through history from them to me, to better-understand the big picture of redemption."

Sue Buchanan
Author, speaker, cheerleader
www. suebue. com

"If you think Bible studies are dull and laborious, think again. Bonnie Keen and Nan Gurley have developed a women's Bible study that is not only going to teach you about the fascinating lives of the women of the Bible, but it will entertain you in the process. Both women are accomplished actors, gifted communicators, and talented entertainers. Their sense of humor, hopeful hearts, and love of teaching come through every page of this study. This is one women's Bible study your group is going to love!"

Martha Bolton
Emmy-nominated writer and author of
over 50 books of humor, including
"Didn't My Skin Used To Fit?"

"Oh, if you have ever longed to have the Bible come alive for you, you are holding the life-changing key in your very hand. This study of God's Word is like none other on the planet! All the dusty stories of long ago have been dusted off and brought into living color. You will discover answers and applications for living your own life with fresh vibrancy and transformed understanding! Open these pages and begin at once to walk in a new sense of personal joy and direction!"

Glenna Salsbury
Christian Conference Speaker and
Author of Heavenly Treasures
ISpeak4U@aol. cocm

"This offering is saturated with raw, buoyant, unconditional love. I ache to see the musical! And I'd encourage all to experience this study. It will be marked by a wondrous marriage of excellence and humanity."

Alicia Britt Chole
"painting portraits of truth that refresh the soul"
www. truthportraits. com

"As I previewed Women Who Dare to Believe, I laughed, wept and marveled at the anointing that is all over this brilliant work! I can't wait to see how God will use the stage performance and the Bible Study to rally His Daughters!"

Candace L. Davison
Women's Ministry Coordinator
Sandy Cove Ministries, North East MD

"Women Who Dare To Believe" reminds us that it is God who lifts and sustains us in this world whatever our time in history. It is so much easier for me to believe in his love for me when I experience the answers to my prayers…just like I prayed them. I dare to believe in the Fathers love even when his good for me hurts. This study reminds me it is only by his Spirit that this is possible. He continues to work mightily in women to bring about his will and to give glory to the Father who made us for so much more than what we see. Go, girls, but only with him."

Nancy Puryear
Director of Women's Ministry
Christ Community Church, Franklin Tn

"Nan Gurley and Bonnie Keen are the real deal. They're as much "women who dare to believe" as any of those described in their studies. Within these pages, expect wit, humor, authenticity, insight, truth, camaraderie, and a fresh look at inspirational lives."

Fiona Soltes, writer, missionary, friend,
and fellow follower of Jesus.

"Bonnie Keen and Nan Gurley have a passion to bring Biblical truth to light. From their wealth of experience and biblical knowledge their latest endeavor "Women Who Dare To Believe" offers a fresh perspective which will encourage and inspire us in our daily walk with the Lord.

Sharleen Dluzak,
Director of Women's Ministry
Church of the Redeemer, Gaithersburg MD

"I have never felt a kindred spirit with women in the Bible till now."

Mary Williams
Great-grandmother and Owner/ President
of Mary Williams Guide Service

"My thanks to the authors for writing this book. I feel like I have had a private, in-depth visit with each woman we studied."

Bernie ArnoldAutor
Mother of 4
Grand Mother of 10

"My wholehearted thanks goes out to Bonnie and Nan for using their God-given gifts to guide mothers, sisters and daughters of our time to know more about His promises. In studying the lives of His chosen women, they dare to create a desire for others to know the depths of God's loving heart."

Gwendolyn Watson

"Our moms wrote this study. It's awesome. Thank goodness it's finished."

Erin and Lena Gurley, Courtney Keen

WELCOME

Disclaimer: This study absolutely, 100 percent, and unapologetically reflects the views of the writers. Please proceed without hesitation no matter your belief system. All are invited. All are welcome. Thank you for your time and attention.

Nan Gurley and Bonnie Keen

You have now entered the highly charged, estrogen-faith-filled world of Bonnie Keen and Nan Gurley. We are grateful to share with you our friendship and the delight we've found through the process of researching the women of God's Word.

Over the course of a thirty-year friendship, we have laughed until we couldn't get off of the floor, screamed with joy at the delight God pours into our lives, cried over lost treasures of the heart, and celebrated as our cups continue to run over. Gratefully married, each with two children, and coming from a posse of siblings, we are quite literally mothers, sisters, and daughters of the living God.

Through the years of our friendship, we have delighted in sharing God stories with each other, telling of his faithfulness in the details of our lives, and sharing the joy of Bible study. We are not biblical scholars, educated in Hebrew and Greek. We are students and practitioners, lovers of our God and of his Word. Our role in writing this study is to shake some of his salt into this world. The purpose of salt is to make you thirsty. We hope you will come away from this experience in the Word thirsty for more. We encourage you to not take our word for anything. Be like the Bereans, who studied the Scriptures to verify the truth for themselves.

Each of us has enjoyed the separate privilege of songwriting, recording, and penning books about our faith in Jesus. This study marks a shared adventure and a new dream.

Women Who Dare to Believe is a joint effort to bring the women in Scripture to life. Some are familiar names, others are less famous. Yet with fresh eyes, deeper review, and a little imagination, perhaps we can take a virtual walk in their shoes. From the pages of the Bible, we listen to hear them call to us from their stories, speaking hope into our own. From the Old Testament to the New, we see our faces mirrored in the struggles of their lives. Their stories are our stories.

The women we highlight in our study exhibited extraordinary strength in a male-dominated culture that gave little credence to a woman's voice. In these pages you will see the most unlikely women emerge to rise up and say, "We will stand strong!" They put everything on the line for their families and always out of a do-or-die belief in Jehovah.

Women who follow after Jesus have a lasting connection, and engage the same challenges no matter the century. We may live in a different time, but upon close inspection, we have the same heart issues. This side of heaven our lives are filled with unexpected twists and turns. Like the women who came before us, we find comfort in serving a faithful God who does not change.

Our prayer is that you find these women of the way fascinating, captivating, and ultimately liberating. Their stories read like the best novel, full of every girl's dreams for acceptance, love, hope, and purpose. These ladies suffered, rejoiced, pushed through, gave up, and gave in to the only God who would love so completely that he gave himself in the person of his son.

We have written this study with the idea of a breaking news story. What if there had been a media machine in existence during the lives of the women in Scripture? How would the headlines have read? Using our sanctified imaginations, we open each week's lesson and character study with the possible headlines of her day, reflecting the history of her situation.

The purpose of looking at our sisters in the Bible through the lens of a current media format is to make their stories more relevant to what we face as women of faith today.

We share the same wear and tear, tears and fears, falling down, getting up, moving on, clinging, and believing. The goal of each weekly lesson is to make these women become very real flesh and blood, warts and all, like ourselves. (Like us, they were far from perfect.) We are connected to them, Jew and Gentile, by our faith in Christ and trust in God. And in Jesus, in spite of everything, nothing can separate us from our heritage as his beloved daughters.

Each chapter is to be completed in one week. Feel free to stop when and where you need to each day, completing the lesson at your own pace. Be prepared to come together at the end of the lesson with other girlfriends to share stories, compare notes, and encourage one another in Jesus.

We have included a list of discussion questions for each lesson at the back of the book. These are meant to spark conversation and give some focus to your time together. You also will find a few suggestions there for anyone who feels led to take more of a leadership or facilitator's role in the group.

Through the power of the Holy Spirit, through the opening of his Word, through your intimate time with him, through meeting old and new girlfriends in the pages of God's history, we pray that you will leave this study with his healing touch on your woman's heart.

We long for you to take your rightful place with us in the ever-growing line of women who dare to believe.

In our risen Jesus we do wildly and continually hope,
most humbled to be on this journey with you,
two of his many beloved daughters!

A SPECIAL THANK YOU

We are grateful to the following women who agreed to be the first to study *Women Who Dare to Believe: Mothers, Sisters, Daughters of God*. Before the Bible study was in the form that you now have, these women graciously opened their Monday night Bible study to us. For five months, they poured their love and energy into doing each lesson and giving us their feedback. Thank you, dear sisters. Your love and encouragement kept us writing and pressing on, believing that you would be the first of many who would come alongside us and dare to believe.

Pat Ward ~ Diana Reed ~ Bernie Arnold ~ Mary Williams ~ Maxine Bivins
Dele Wilcher ~ Becky Collins ~ Betsy Piper ~ Irene Acuff ~ Debbie Costantine ~ Eva Crothers ~
Jeannie Boshers ~ Glenda Cowart ~ Renee Crawford

World News

PRO-LIFE MIDWIVES' UNION STANDS STRONG, DEFIES GOVERNMENT MANDATE

Pharaoh's Diet Plan for Hebrews Is To Die For

Forecast: Perpetually hot conditions. Sunny. 120 degrees.

Pollen Count: 0.

Possibility of Precipitation: 0.

Humidity level: 0.

For generations, descendants from the twelve tribes of Israel have enjoyed favored status under Egypt's rule. This was due in large part to Joseph's role in Egypt's illustrious history. During Joseph's stay in the capital, he was second in command of Egypt's government, shoring up the nation's food supply during a seven-year drought. His skill not only saved Egypt from starvation but also enriched its national treasury in the process.

Presently for the Hebrews this blanket of protection has completely unraveled.

Under our new administration, the reigning Pharaoh expressed alarm at the growing population of Hebrews. The God of this Israelite nation has obviously blessed them in number and health. To combat their increasing presence, Pharaoh issued the following statement:

"There are way too many of these Israelites for us to handle. We've got to do something: Let's devise a plan to contain them, lest if there's a war they should join our enemies, or just walk off and leave us"

(Exod. 1:9-10 The Message).

Living in the ghetto of Goshen, the people of Israel have been under back-breaking rule, building storage cities of Pithom and Rameses. Yet the latest census shows the nation continues to flourish.

In a strikingly bold move, Pharaoh has issued an official mandate for the already enslaved nation. *World News* has learned that Shiphrah and Puah, two leaders of the Midwives' Union, were put under direct orders to kill all Hebrew male babes at birth.

In a shocking act of insubordination, the midwives refused to carry out these orders. Enraged by their stand for life, Pharaoh demanded an explanation.

The midwives issued the following statement earlier today:

"We respect God far more than any government and have chosen to let

the children live. God gives life and only he can take it away." The midwives then added, "It's not our fault that the Hebrew women are so strong! Often when we're called, the baby has already been delivered and whisked away by the time we arrive."

Not only are the numbers of Hebrew babies growing; oddly enough, so are the numbers of marriages and babies born to the midwives. This bold pro-life stance from the union has further enraged the king as he appears powerless in the shadow of their God. Overriding his previous order to the Midwives Union, the following mandate has been issued:

"By order of the government, to all residents in Egypt: Every Hebrew boy that is born must be thrown into the Nile River. Every girl, however, may live."

Remember your leaders who spoke the word of God to you. Consider the outcome of their way of life and imitate their faith. Jesus is the same yesterday and today and forever. Heb. 13:7-8 NIV

TODAY'S HEROINES:
The Midwives of Egypt

Read Exodus 2:1-3.

Picture this: In the blistering noonday sun, as the heat rises from the streets of the slave ghetto, a Hebrew woman cries out in the final stages of labor. She is comforted by her teen-age daughter and a woman from the midwife's guild who is coaching her through labor and encouraging her to push. This agony soon will be over, but another one will take its place. If she gives birth to a son, he will be taken from her before she can even wipe the sweat from her face and hold him to her breast. He quickly will be taken from her arms and thrown into the Nile River, where he will drown or become food for the crocodiles. She tries to stifle her cries of pain. Spies walk the streets, listening for the sounds of labor and the first cry of a newborn. She is praying for a girl child.

Thus begins a moment in time when four women will come to a crossroads: a midwife, a mother, a big sister, and a princess. All will be asked to make a difficult choice. No matter what they choose, the road will not be an easy one.

The midwives: Read Exodus 1:17-22.

Into this picture God has sent a courageous woman to help this mother keep her baby alive. She is no ordinary midwife. The midwife who stands beside her at the birthing stool is one who fears the living God more than the current law of the land and will risk her own life before she will deliver this child to his death.

9

The baby is born. It is a boy.

In the first book of Exodus we may well have come upon the first pro-life movement recorded in history. Exodus 1 describes an edict from a paranoid pharaoh who ordered the murder of all Hebrew male newborns. This is the first biblical account of civil disobedience.

The Word of God is filled with stories of women who dared to believe God and obey him in the face of overwhelming danger. Like the slow beat of a drum, we read the opening chapters of Exodus and find ourselves caught up in the high drama and brave faith of some of God's most intriguing women. Not far into the first chapter the drumbeat centers on one tiny beat of a human heart.

What captures the heart of any woman?

What can unite women from completely different backgrounds, ages and income brackets?

A baby.

Find a baby in the Bible, find a barren woman, or find a woman who faces danger for her family, and you'll find God is about to show himself mighty and his promises unchanged. Find a baby in the Bible and you'll find God's agent for deliverance.

It is a moment of destiny for everyone in the room. These women must choose between God's future for this baby and Pharaoh's plan for his life. Either choice brings great risk. There is a holocaust for male babies occurring in this land. To defy the king's law and save this child will be dangerous for both women. They must weigh the personal cost and decide to stand, one way or the other.

Have you ever seen the names of these midwives? We don't know for sure if they were Hebrew or Egyptian. Their names were Shiphrah, which means "beautiful one," and Puah, which means "splendid one." When Moses wrote his memoirs, he included their names and left out the name of the pharaoh! We love it! How highly esteemed these women were, not only in the eyes of the Hebrews, but also in God's eyes. Under the inspiration of the Holy Spirit, God guided Moses' hand many years later as he wrote the story and included the names of these two courageous women. How Moses must have smiled when he wrote their names. When he was grown, we're sure he made it his business to find out who was responsible for helping him stay alive.

Do you wonder if he ever met them again? It is possible they were still alive when Moses led the Hebrews out of Egypt. They would have been well advanced in years by then, with children and grandchildren of their own. We like to picture a moment with Moses and the brave midwives. For Shiphrah and Puah, it would have been a proud moment of looking at the one who stood before Pharaoh and became the mouthpiece of God on behalf of their people. They would have been thrilled to know they had a huge part in the fulfillment of Moses' destiny. And they would have been so thankful that Yahweh had given them the courage to stand in those horrible days.

And what would Moses have said to them? What words of gratitude would he have spoken to the ones who stood by his mother and helped keep him alive? It's fun to imagine. Moses would have held them and their descendants in high esteem.

By the time the midwives were summoned and ordered to kill all newborn Hebrew males, the previous pharaoh from the book of Genesis was safely embalmed in his pyramid tomb. Some things never change: History can be quickly forgotten.

Next, read Exodus 1:6-14.

Exodus 1:8 describes a new pharaoh who did not know Joseph. Too bad he hadn't looked through the vaults of history to read about the life of Joseph and how God's favor fell on Egypt during years of famine and drought. It might have calmed the threatening insecurity that inspired a killing spree.

From a family of seventy immigrants, God blessed twelve tribes to build a nation. His promise to increase their numbers as grains of sand and stars in heaven was playing out before the Egyptian king. He was terrified. If they continued to grow in number they might become a military threat by joining any enemy opposing Egypt.

Step one: Birth control.

The king put the Hebrews on an extreme slave worker diet: long hours, low calories, no protein, lots of high fiber (as in straw), lifting bricks, and construction of government buildings. How frustrated the king must have been. He was enraged to see that even cruel slavery didn't decrease the birth rate or weaken their people.

Step two: Call in the midwives.

What is the most striking aspect of Exodus 1:15-17?

_____

_____

Let's have a little fun. You and your best friend are the two midwives. Each of you has received a subpoena demanding your presence before the king. This man is the ruler of the known world. How much time would you have between the summons and the moment you stand before him? What would you and your friend have worn to the Egyptian throne room? Most definitely you would not have dressed to kill. Imagine you're on the steps of the palace. You've already put two and two together and know this is not going to be good. You grab the hand of your friend, knowing you may not leave alive. This king is a known, vicious racist and anti-Semite. He knows what you do for a living. He hates the people you work for, the ones who gave you special names of honor. You know he's not calling you in to offer you a raise. You are every Hebrew mother's best friend. You are the one they call on to guide them through childbirth. You are strong for them when they're in pain, holding their hands through the process. You cut the umbilical cord and your hands are the first to touch their child and lay it on their breast.

You love what you do and you're not about to change. You know it's politically incorrect to be pro-life.

The guards come to escort you into Pharaoh's office. You hold each other's hands, remembering the pact you made to not look around, appear nervous, or let these powerful surroundings intimidate you. Suddenly you are the only two women in a room of ruthless politicians, including the king of the civilized world.

Your hands feel clammy and you fight back fear. Pharaoh doesn't even look you in the eye before getting right to his point. Things are about to change in your workplace. The next time either of you is called to deliver a Hebrew child, if it is a boy, you are to kill the child as it is being born. You feel your friend's quick intake of breath. Neither of you speak. Neither can believe what you hear. By order of the king you are to perform what he calls "late-term abortion." As you leave the palace you must make a decision that will endanger your lives.

You and your friend don't know it at the time, but the choice you make this day will be told to generations to come. It will inspire little boys named Shadrach, Meshach and Abednego and a future queen named Esther.

Your chance to offer an editorial: Write the conversation the midwives may have had leaving the palace. (If you're doing this with your best friend, save this exercise for when you are together.)

_____

_____

_____

These courageous midwives did not kill the babies. Could it be that stories of God's faithfulness had been told year after year, especially during the 400 years of silence between Genesis and Exodus? How important it is to keep telling our children of the Lord's promises.

The midwives had no Torah to give them strength. But the stories of the Lord were passed down from generation to generation. They knew in the deepest part of their hearts that even though the rule of Egypt may have changed, Jehovah God was in control and would capture their yesterdays, give them strength for their todays, and bless their tomorrows.

Read Exodus 1:18-22.

What happened to the midwives because of their disobedience to the king?

_____

_____

Don't you love this? They feared God more than the world power of their time. And God blessed them with their own baby showers and children of their own. Pharaoh must have been throwing a fit by the time he ordered all the people of Egypt to throw newborn male sons into the Nile.

Step three: Order everyone, everywhere, to kill the babies.

Another failed order from Egypt's throne.

Most of the time we know the right thing to do, we just lack the courage to do it. How does their courage inspire you?

_____

_____

_____

Need a shot of courage? Read these passages and choose your favorite to memorize. Write it on an index card and keep it close: a little biblical Vitamin "C" for Courage.

Proverbs 28:1; 2 Timothy 1:7; Daniel 3:16-18; Acts 5:29; Ezekiel 2:6; Esther 4:16; Acts 20:22-24; Philippians 1:27-28.

With none of the scriptures above, these two midwives helped safely birth the Hebrew boys of Egypt. And on this particular day, they helped deliver the one who would deliver the Hebrew nation out of slavery. They guarded the one who would forever be a foreshadowing of the one who would deliver all humanity.

We're all called to be a midwife to something. What about you? What are you helping bring forth into life? Are you interceding for the spiritual life of a loved one? Are you vigilantly shepherding your talents and the work he has called you to do? What are you guarding?

The enemy of our souls would gladly see the hope within us die. Like the crocodiles in the Nile, he is waiting to devour our dreams. If we are going to successfully midwife the destiny and works God has prepared for us since the foundation of the world, then it will require us to be vigilant. It will call us to defy anyone and everything that seeks to steal from us. Put on your armor. Stand up and stand tall. We're going to have to answer to God one day about how we guarded our treasures. Don't disdain the day of small things and fall into the trap of thinking your work is too insignificant to matter. In the faithfulness of your ordinary days, you are participating in great things.

Take a moment to read Ephesians 2:10.

What are the dreams that God wants you to bring to life and protect while they grow? Make a list of some things God has entrusted to you.

GOD HAS ENTRUSTED TO ME:

1.

2.

3.

4.

5.

Prepare to be challenged as you walk in obedience. Prepare to be questioned for the stand you take, and for the dreams you nurture that you know to be God's leading even when people don't understand. As a midwife, what do you need from God in order to safely deliver what he has entrusted to you back into his hands one day?

_____

_____

Every courageous woman who follows hard after God is able to pass that courage on to another. On the heels of the story of the midwives, we will study the amazing courage of Jochebed. Take heart from the faith of the midwives from ancient Egypt. Like them, we can hold fast to the same God who protected them in a world turning upside down.

Take a moment to think about the Shiphrahs or Puahs in your personal history, women who have encouraged and nurtured you by their examples of faith. Write their names here:

_____

_____

The Bible tells us that God honored Puah and Shiphrah them for their obedience and "provided households for them" (Exod. 1:21 NKJV). It was typical back then for a household to be established for men only. In this situation, God let the houses be established in the names of Puah and Shiphrah. These women feared God instead of Pharaoh. Their courage and willingness to risk the possibility of their own deaths in order to defy the king won them great favor with God.

Your faithful vigilance in the face of opposition is what you are called to do. It is a holy work. We're surprised sometimes by all the things that constantly push against our efforts to walk in faithfulness, everything from outright attack from the enemy to our own selfishness and sinful nature. But if it wasn't so important, it would be easy. Why would satan want to derail something that didn't matter? So when you feel the pressure, remember that it's normal and that it must be eternally significant, or satan wouldn't care. That's something to chew on!

TODAY'S DATE: _____

PERSONALIZE TODAY'S HEADLINE: Dream with God about how you are going to change the future by your choices today!

_____

_____

"Don't be afraid of tomorrow. God is already there."
- *Charles Spurgeon*

𝕳ebrew 𝕲azette

~Underground Newspaper~

Egypt, 1527 B. C

Editor's warning:
Any Israelite caught with the Hebrew Gazette will be considered dangerous and punishable by Egyptian law.

MOTHERS OF NEWBORN MALES STAND STRONG

In response to the mandated deaths of our newborn sons, we pray for each family who must decide how to respond in protecting your children. While Egypt may see the lives of our sons as a threat or inconvenience, we know that Jehovah God gives life to our nation through their births.

Remember the actions of Noah. God provided an ark to deliver Noah's family during the flood. Remember Abraham. When asked to lay down his son, Isaac, God provided the ram. Mothers, stand strong. Think outside the box. Be creative.

Our Lord is with you.

Draw me out of the net that they have laid secretly for me, for You are my Strength and my Stronghold. Ps. 31:4 Amplified Bible

TODAY'S HEROINE:
Jochebed, mother of Moses

Read Exodus 2:1-3.

As the midwife stands over Jochebed and encourages her to push, what is going through this mother's mind? If her baby is a son, what will she do? This was the third child for Amram and his wife Jochebed. Their eldest was a daughter named Miriam, followed by a son, Aaron. And finally, three years later, in a climate of extreme danger came the arrival of their youngest, another son.

When Jochebed was in labor with Moses, the Hebrew children were a mere eighty years away from throwing off the chains of slavery and beginning their journey into the joy and freedom of the Promised Land.

But no one knows this as she labors on the birthing stool. When Moses was born, all anyone could see was a never-ending future of oppression, heartache, forced labor, and now infanticide. None of them knew that deliverance would come through his life. All they could do was put one weary foot in front of the other and try to survive another day.

Into this setting, a woman named Jochebed gives birth to a baby boy. Something even beyond her loving eyes of motherhood could see this child was special. She risks all to save him from the Egyptian police. How could she keep this baby alive? Could she hide him indefinitely? What were the risks to her other children? To herself, to her husband?

Pharaoh viewed all Hebrew boys as potential enemies. The Hebrew population was outnumbering the Egyptians. If he could not enslave them all, then he would not permit them to grow up and one day threaten him.

How could Jochebed keep Egyptian neighbors and spies from hearing her baby's cries? Her stress level had to be unbearable. Newborns cry and squeal; they smile and coo. They cuddle their fingers around their mother as she nurses them in the night. They stretch and yawn, make funny faces, and look like angels as they sleep. The bond between a mother and her new infant is the strongest bond on the face of the earth.

Jochebed must have come to the conclusion that if her beloved son would die, it would not be without a fight. Mustering courage only a mother can understand, she prepared a basket for her babe. Never able to take him out in public, she kept him hidden and quiet until, one day, the plan was put into action.

Imagine for a moment what lengths you'd go to, to save your own children, grandchildren, or any child put in your care. What are the greatest threats to children in our culture?

_____

_____

_____

In Proverbs 6:17-19, we find a list of the things God hates. Turn there and read verse 17 aloud.

Lest we feel Jochebed's measures to save her son were a bit hormonal, maybe too drastic, glance through some recent statistics about the children living in the twenty-first century:

More than one million children become involved in sex trade each year.
More than one million children live and work on the streets of our world's megacities.
One third of the world's population is under the age of fifteen, and more than 200,000 of these are fighting in wars. [1]
Three thousand babies are aborted each day in the United States. [2]

We all could use a shot of encouragement right now. **Turn to Psalm 127:3, take a deep breath, and remember God's deep love for the life of a child versus the way children are treated in our world.**

"Behold, children are a heritage from the Lord, the fruit of the womb a reward" (Amplified Bible).

God doesn't see human life in terms of statistics; he sees each life as a reward. He takes what happens to them extremely personally. Murder and mistreatment of the innocent rank in the top seven things which he hates! Lives are not numbers in a poll, or lines on a graph. *Nelson's New Illustrated Bible Commentary* reads: "The word "hates" progresses to "abomination." The word "abomination" is the Bible's strongest expression of hatred for wickedness." [3]

It's good to remember we serve a passionate God at the turning of our new century. We don't live in Egypt in 2,000 B.C. Yet do we mothers today voice some of the same sentiments of this Hebrew mother? "This is a crazy time to have children! Look at the condition of our world, the dangers, diseases, godless nations, challenges my family will have to face. Will they make it safely through teen-age years, and what then? Only by entrusting them to God can I keep hope alive." Our children are born into the safe, secure world of our arms. But before we know it, step by step they go walking into the unknown, threatening, real world.

Bulrushes come in every shape, size and variety.

I (Bonnie) have a daughter and son. I know the ecstatic joy of motherhood. The months of pregnancy filled with wonder as I watched my body change. The first tiny butterfly movements that gradually turned into full kicks to the ribs. The waves of nausea that meant the baby was pulling the nutrients it needed from the marrow of my bones. The anticipation. *What would this child be like? A boy? A girl? Would I be a good mother?*

I know full well the labor pangs (albeit I went for the epidural both times). After hours of pushing and panting, praying for my child to be healthy and whole, at last the miracle of seeing Courtney, my daughter! Four and half years later, the sheer joy of birthing Graham, my son! With that first sound of their cries, the first touch of their bodies on mine, I was instantly, forever, and hopelessly in love.

A mother's heart is defenseless. The Momma Bear instinct is primal and intense. And nothing is as profoundly sad as attending the burial of a child. Several unforgettable times I've attended a baby's memorial service. Just the sight of a tiny casket shook me to my core.

18

So it's impossible for me to wrap myself in the skin of Jochebed, this brave Hebrew mother. I delivered my children in the safety of a sterile, nurse-laden American hospital room. She faced pregnancy and birth with the looming threat of a death sentence for her child. What did she think when she saw her third child was a son? Did she secretly hope it would be a girl baby, guaranteeing safety from Egypt's sword?

Read Exodus 2:3 again and answer the following question:

How do you imagine Jochebed hid her son during the first three months?

_____

_____

Jochebed was living in a time when the highest ruler of the land believed himself to be a god in the flesh. Talk about ego. How do you reason with that? She could not rely on anyone in government to be fair in regard to the sanctity of life. She was at the mercy of a ruthless despot bent on annihilating every Hebrew male child. In the bitterness of the times, did she wonder, *Where is God in all this? Has he forgotten me? Does he see me? Does he know what I'm dealing with here?*

If Pharaoh wanted to break the spirit of the Hebrew people, this was a good way to do it. He made murder of the Hebrew boys a matter of public policy. He deputized everyone in Egypt to join the police force and to look for male Hebrew children. Any citizen in the land was authorized to take a Hebrew baby from its mother and throw him into the Nile. How curious that as Jochebed made a plan for Moses, she chose the Nile as a place to hide him. She put him in this place of death and dared to trust that God would come through for her. She knew something about God that made her take the risk to trust him with her son.

In the midst of this unthinkable injustice, we would have found it difficult to calm down enough to make a plan. Rage at the inhuman treatment and the wicked people in power would have driven us mad.

Where do you put this kind of anger? What do you do with it so it doesn't destroy you? If there had been an underground newspaper circulating in the ghetto homes of the Hebrews, it would have recalled the salvation of the family of Noah, the deliverance of the promised child named Isaac, the favor of a prisoner named Joseph. It had been 400 years, but we have to wonder if she did not lose heart because of the memory of Joseph, saved from death by a rescuing God who provided a way.

Somehow Jochebed took a deep breath and found courage. She took matters out of her own hands and placed them in the unseen hands of God. The Nile River would be the most out-of-control, vulnerable, and unprotected scenario to the human eye. Were the crocodiles hungry that day? By faith, Jochebed placed her baby in a situation she could not control and trusted God that Moses would land exactly where God wanted him to be.

We can't help but stop here a moment and ask: Is there something we need to let go of and launch into unseen waters? Life seems to be a series of difficult moments of letting go. We enjoy the sense of control over the things that matter most to us. Jochebed took her most treasured and vulnerable possession and let it go. We don't know how she did it.

Everything we're given must be given back to him, held loosely, allowed to go into places we may never have chosen, but he ordained. In the letting go, we launch our treasures and offer them back.

What can you do today to prepare for the letting go?

Turn to Hebrews 13:5b. What promises do we have from God about our circumstances?

_____

_____

_____

Now turn to Deuteronomy 6:4-9. This parenting how-to guide offers us several helpful instructions. Based on this passage, write a short how-to version for your life.

_____

_____

_____

_____

_____

Tell your story, as Jochebed would tell hers, or as Miriam would write in her journal. Your story has the same elements of God-drenched drama: risk, destiny, choices, consequences, understanding of the times, courage, and trusting God in all of it. What connected these women? A helpless baby boy, and the choice to do the right thing.

Our own stories may not seem as dramatic, but they still matter to our children. They need to hear about what God has done and is doing in our lives to keep our families together, our faith working, our hearts beating with hope.

One wonders what Jochebed was thinking as she forced herself to lay her infant son in a tiny boat, tears falling onto his outstretched arms, tucking a blanket around his legs. Was he smiling as if Momma was playing a fun new game? She might have said, "God blessed the midwives for their obedience. God blesses. God gives life. God, keep the waters calm today. God, keep me from coming apart. God, be where I cannot go." It's hard to imagine she didn't retell her story to baby Moses in the days and months, perhaps years, to come.

Did Miriam help her mom with the difficult sendoff? Or perhaps try to talk some sense into her mother's crazy plan? Miriam had the first-born syndrome to deal with, and a few hormones thrown in as well. More about that later.

This much we do know: Jochebed's courage in Jehovah saved her son. Miriam's courage to obey her mother's orders to follow the tiny ark brought God's blessing. Like mother, like daughter, the red blood of faith flowed through their veins, and their hearts must have been about to burst with emotion. Imagine the prayers rushing to heaven for this helpless little babe.

It's interesting to note that Jochebed was from the tribe of Levi. This tribe was later chosen to be priests that ministered to the Lord in the tabernacle and in the tent of meeting. I am sure it pleased the heart of our Father when she trusted him with the destiny of her baby boy. Just like the Levites, every act of trust rises like incense before the Lord, a fragrant offering of faith that is accounted to us as righteousness.

Read Psalm 141:2 and Revelation 8:3-4.

Does it thrill your heart to know that even prayers we feel don't make it much past the kitchen ceiling rise as fragrance to our God? Write a simple prayer below!

_____

_____

_____

Maybe Jochebed recalled the faith of the midwives. Did she attend the celebrations for their children? We'll have to ask her all about it when we meet her in heaven.

At this moment in her history, it was a time of extreme persecution for the people of God. They were completely out of favor with the governing powers of the day. Yet the harsher the treatment, the more they flourished.

The Egyptians feared the Israelites. The enemy of our soul fears the people that God holds dear. That's hard, because the enemy works to make our lives miserable. Are you oppressed? You are stronger than you realize. You are a child of God and you have his favor on you. The enemy is afraid of you. A sold-out child of God is his worst nightmare.

How do we behave under pressure? Are we flourishing? Is our spirit broken? That's what the enemy desires. Don't fall into his trap and decide God has forgotten you. Don't give up. Press on in faith.

Take heart in the courageous stories of other mothers living in different times in history who shared the same fears we have and chose the path of bold faith in God.

I (Nan) have the privilege of being the mother of two adopted daughters from China. Erin and Lena are the most glorious blessings of my life. During the process of endless paperwork and waiting for our trip to China to bring them home, I learned all I could about the plight of Chinese mothers and their children.

I learned about the one-child-per-family law in China and how most families want boys instead of girls. The reason for this is because in Chinese culture, the sons never leave home. They marry and bring their wives into their parents' home, thus taking care of the parents in their old age. It is the Chinese version of social security.

When a Chinese mother finds herself pregnant, she knows she's only got one chance to raise a child. So she prays for a boy.

In many cases, when a girl is born, the mother will take the infant daughter to a public place and walk away. She is hoping the baby will be noticed, picked up, and taken to a police station. From there, the child will be placed in an orphanage.

Often, there will be a red note pinned to the daughter's clothing or blanket. It is on red paper because the Chinese believe the color red brings good luck. The note will have the baby's birthday on it and a mother's heartfelt wish that her daughter will have a good life. It is the mother's last effort to send her child into the future with love and hope for the child's life.

EDITORIAL: Write a note Jochebed may have placed in the ark/basket with her tiny child.

_____

_____

_____

_____

_____

Here's what I imagine she might have written:

"To my most beautiful child, beloved of my heart. I do not know where this tiny boat will take you, but God knows. Wherever you go, my heart goes too. Whatever you do in this life, you will have my greatest prayers, my deepest desires for strength, and daily offering of you to our God. Know him, my dear. He will keep you safe in his hands. He knit you together in my body, and knows every path you will walk. Into his hands and only his can I bear to let you go. In his time, I pray to hold you in my arms again. They will ache and long for you until the day I die. Jehovah God, watch over my beloved."

Jochebed placed her infant son in a basket, in a river of death and sent him into the direction of danger. Only a desperate momma would send this tiny ark toward Egypt. Only a desperate act of faith would keep him alive.

Read Psalm 139:12-16.

As a mom, or aunt, or mentor of a child, which verse comforts you the most?

_____

_____

_____

Courtney and Graham (Bonnie's kids) are young adults now. But when I look up at them (up from my five-foot-eleven-inch height) I still see the children I raised. Now they walk through bulrushes of a different kind.

I cannot be there to dry tears, protect them from injustice, or make their choices. Parenthood is a slow, bittersweet process of letting go. Presently, Courtney moved from Alabama to Denver and then had the good sense to move back to Nashville where I live. Graham is in New York City working on a musical theater degree. Talk about some bulrushes and crocodiles!

In their lifetimes, they've seen the horrors of a Columbine massacre, the unthinkable tragedy of September 11, 2001. They were very young when I found myself a single mom, divorced and depressed, trying to find enough faith to believe my children would know God in spite of their circumstances. Thanks be to God for being father, mother, provider, and the lover of their souls. Both Courtney and Graham love Jesus, and know God has their back, side, front, and everything in between.

One passage we cling to as mothers is Isaiah 44:2-4. Please go there now.

What promise do we find in **verses 3 and 4**?

_____

_____

_____

Yes, God will pour his Spirit onto our offspring and his blessing upon our descendants. Thankfully he does the pouring; he does the blessing.

We know the end of the story. God honored Jochebed's faith and he saved her baby boy. But at the time, she had no idea how it would all turn out. For all she knew, her baby would never make it. Maybe she thought, *If he's going to die, at least it won't be by the hand of a ruthless stranger.* Or she may have launched his little ark right where she knew the royal house of Egypt enjoyed bathing. But one look under the diaper was all the evidence the Egyptian princess would need to know it was a Hebrew baby. A circumcised male infant was doomed.

Whatever Jochebed's plan was, she was walking by faith. That always gets the attention of heaven. Are you in the process of letting go of something very dear to you? If you are, then trust that God is very near, and that he is waiting to receive your treasure.

Whenever we are tempted to fear the rushing rivers facing our babes, we remember the faithful mercy of God over our lives. Many times we sense the Holy Spirit quiet our mother's hearts with these questions: *Was God there for you when you made your way? Was he in the bulrushes with you? Did he deliver you out of your own mess? Has he changed? Is he big enough, strong, and full of grace for your children?* Yes, we quietly exhale. God will be where we cannot go. Like Jochebed, we have a choice to trust him with the treasures of our hearts.

Soon a princess of Egypt would rescue the babe and name him Moses. Pharaoh's daughter explains the meaning of the name: "because I drew him out of the water."[4] Moved by a God she did not worship, she spoke prophetically over this Hebrew son who would one day draw the Israelite nation out of bondage. **In reflecting on the high drama of this story, reread today's verse from Psalm 31:4.**

"Draw me out of the net they have laid secretly for me, for You are my Strength and my Stronghold" (Amplified Bible).

Jochebed trusted God beyond what she could see. She believed God would draw her son out of the net of danger and into a place of safety. She wasn't living in "lala land." She was immersed in a climate of immediate death threats. But she knew her God was her strength! Trust him today with what you cannot see. She believed her son had a future in spite of the law of the land. We serve the same God. Believe him for your children. Believe in spite of the enemy's lies, in spite of yourself, even in spite of your circumstances or theirs. Your children are his!

TODAY'S DATE: _____

PERSONALIZE TODAY'S HEADLINE:

_____

What bulrushes do your children face? What does the present culture want to steal from your child? How has Jochebed's story renewed your faith in God's sovereign plan for your family? Our world sits waiting for a new generation of children to grow up and into their faith in an unchanging Lord. We have the breathtaking gift of praying, believing, and daring to trust God with a new line of deliverers!

Local Life & Entertainment

Teen-Age Runaway Rescued From Nile

In a bizarre tale of search and rescue, a young teen-age Hebrew girl was discovered by the royal princess and returned to her parents. Unofficial reports will only release her first name: Miriam. Apparently Miriam is one in a long line of many Hebrew runaways. By all accounts she hoped to blend into Egypt's culture and escape the backbreaking work of her people. Though none can blame these teen-age runaways, it is disheartening to note the growing trend toward lack of respect for their families.

From her private bathhouse, Egypt's princess saw Miriam wandering aimlessly down the crocodile-infested waters of the Nile. In an act of mercy, the princess spoke with the teen-ager who had lost track of her belongings. The young lady was found in possession of a small basket assumed to carry her clothes and belongings.

After a brief encounter with the princess, Miriam returned home, her basket in tow. One can only speculate as to what greater harm she may have encountered, posed by the reptilian threats of the Nile. Our great princess is known for acts of kindness and grace, thus continuing her noble representation of Egypt's character to even the most underprivileged in the land.

Parents, please talk to your children. Keep an open line of communication. If they show any signs of isolation, depression, abnormal behavior or substance abuse, please take advantage of all government social services made available by our great Pharoah.

And the Lord answered: Can a woman forget her nursing child, that she should not have compassion on the son of her womb? Yes, they may forget, yet I will not forget you.
Isa. 49:15 Amplified Bible

TODAY'S HEROINE:
Miriam, sister of Moses

Read Exodus 2:4-7.

When Miriam waded into waters of the Nile to follow a basket holding her three-month-old brother, she was a young maiden, the Hebrew term for a woman of marriageable age. Did she have any sense that the whole world did not rest on her beautiful young shoulders?

Miriam's role in this story is an odd one. Did she think her mother's plan was a good one? We can picture her, the big sister, perhaps going day after day, standing in the muddy waters of the Nile thinking to herself, *What am I doing in these bulrushes?* How many days has she done this? Her mother has told her to babysit Moses in the deep water and wait until the royal family comes to the riverbank. She hopes today will be the day that the royal women come down to do their ritual bathing. She hopes they'll be in a good mood.

From what little we know, Miriam had faith. It was the kind of faith that supersedes worry over the future. Faith that believes God will protect ankles, knees, wrists, bodies from a raging river filled with danger. Faith in a God who has a plan. Faith in the request of a desperate mother who might just have a holy clue.

Obviously Miriam knew about the deaths of infant baby boys. She may have witnessed their murders and heard the weeping of mothers in her neighborhood. The throne of Egypt demanded their deaths. Every Hebrew male baby was a perceived threat to the world government.

Yet, in this atmosphere of imminent threat to life and limb, Miriam walked into the waters of the Nile to watch over her brother. We wonder if she might have relished the often-quoted words of Corrie ten Boom, a twentieth-century survivor of another Holocaust:

"Faith is like radar that sees through the fog—the reality of things at a distance that the human eye cannot see."

Miriam had no compass, no radar in the fog to illuminate the path of her young brother's life. But she shines like a beacon of blazing light in the pages of ancient history. She pulled up her skirts and waded in, laying aside whatever dreams she had for her future, choosing to see where the river would lead.

Let's take a moment to walk in her sandals.

This young Hebrew teen-ager was the oldest child of an enslaved family. Miriam would have been somewhere in her mid- to late teens. Do you remember this age? Hormones pushing against dreams against reason to birth hope? History does little to change the rites and passages of womanhood. Was she that different from any other young lady?

Imagine being Miriam's age, in the prime of her beauty and insecurity. Add to this mix the threats of death to her brother's life if his giggles and cries were heard in the night. Did she wrestle somewhere between: *Baby brother, shut up!* and *Dear Lord, what will happen to us now?* Top off this tension with a firstborn's sense of responsibility. Miriam was one tough little daughter of God.

I (Bonnie) am the eldest daughter of the eldest daughter of an eldest daughter. My first-born is a girl, and so the story goes. Matriarchs march through my heritage and I have learned to watch for the pros and cons of this legacy. It's not easy being a firstborn, no matter the gender. We tend toward people pleasing. We are Type A people and push hard to make our mark on the world. For whatever reason, firstborns feel a shade more responsibility than the siblings that follow.

Stan, my younger brother by three years, suffered through many of my big-sister rants. I bossed him around, directed him in "plays" in spite of his protests, and wrestled him to the ground until finally he was too big and there was a power shift. Amy, seven years younger, was like a play toy, my doll to dress up and spoil. Poor Stan and I duked it out more, but I love them both with all my heart and would have duked it out with anyone who tried to hurt either of them.

How grateful I am that Stan has forgiven me for many a big-sister blunder. (Space doesn't permit my defense of the details of when I backed him into a corner, resulting in a broken collarbone. His. I digress.) Presently, we laugh until we cry, recalling memories that only family members can truly appreciate.

But I was no match for Miriam. If only I had been this kind of older sister! I love my younger brother and sister, case closed. But if my mother told me to follow Stan's little basket into a river infested with all manner of creepy crawly reptiles I know I would have run in the opposite direction. If she had suggested I watch from the bulrushes to see where he landed, I might have come down with a spontaneous case of the flu. Forget that plan! My teen-age brain would have been all over any and every excuse to excuse myself.

Let's be clear here: Bulrushes were ten to fifteen feet tall and as thick as three inches. Replace the Bible Story "cute" pictorials of Miriam wading among some lovely, green weeds. This girl was filled with fierce faith. She walked into a threatening river. The currents of the river alone could have swept her away. But something in her young faith gave her legs of steel. Most people wouldn't take on crocodiles, snakes, unpredictable currents, and towering reeds unless a TV camera promised to roll for a new reality show.

In spite of it all, this teen-age sister obeyed her mother's wishes, and waded into the dangerous waters of the Nile. With no *Big-Sister Survival Manual for Dummies*, Miriam simply obeyed. We read her story, hold our breath, and are astonished at her strength.

Not only did she wade down the river, but this gutsy young lady was not afraid to make herself known. When the princess picked up her baby brother, Miriam's mind must have raced. To speak or not to speak, that was the question. Here's another:

"Shall I go and get one of the Hebrew women to nurse the baby for you?" (Exod. 2:7 NIV)

What kind of protocol do you imagine Miriam broke by approaching the princess with such an offer?

_____

_____

Would this teen-age slave girl even have the right to speak to the Egyptian royal family? Who knows all the danger Miriam risked? Her profound request had tremendous implications. List a few that come to mind.

1.

2.

3.

Our list would be:

1. To involve the princess would be implying she was going to take care of the babe.
2. To involve a Hebrew woman to nurse him would involve her mother.
3. By involving both women, Miriam and her baby brother would be spared death.

Quite an impressive young girl, this Miriam!

Wouldn't you love to have been one of the attendants that day, watching and wondering about the conversation between this princess of royal power and the young teen-age girl? Did anyone know that world events shifted that day all because of a tiny, helpless baby? They did, and all because of the common connection of woman to woman, determined to save a life.

Miriam's assignment was a messy job and a risky one. She doesn't know it at the time but when her brother grows up, he will lead the Hebrew nation into the desert and out of slavery. And in the future, her life will once again be one of serving him.

As we fast forward for a moment in the coming years of history, Miriam would face even more danger and challenges as his eldest sibling. We wonder if she felt a little overlooked. When Moses was in his full power as leader of Israel, did she want to say, "Hey, remember me? I changed your diapers. I risked my life for you, for heaven's sake. And if it weren't for me, your little behind would still be stuck in the bulrushes! So show a little respect!"

Turn to Numbers 12:1-2 and read.

Here's quite a different scenario. Imagine Miriam and Aaron behaving like that. They both seem to resent Moses' authority. They seem to feel less than appreciated. Can you identify? We can.

Do you ever feel invisible? Are there not many people who appreciate you? Then look to Miriam and take heart, dear daughter. Your quiet and unseen walk of obedience and worship is highly esteemed in heaven. One of our favorite passages describes a heavenly accounting of our faithfulness.

Let's turn to Malachi 3:14-18.

What were the people saying in **verse 14**?

_____

_____

What was God's reaction to their opinion of the worth of obedience and faithfulness?

_____

_____

How much did they think it was worth doing the right thing each day?

_____

_____

In **verse 16**, what did those who feared the Lord do when they were together?

_____

_____

What was God's response to their conversations?

_____

_____

According to **verse 18**, what will one day be evident to all?

_____

_____

If you feel your quiet faithfulness goes unnoticed by God, take heart. His Word promises that there are ongoing conversations in heaven right now about you. They are not gossipy words of condemnation, accusing you of one little failure or another. They are words of delight every time you choose to believe. Do you revere him? Do you worship him? Then believe, dear daughter, your faithful words and deeds are actually written down in a book in the library of heaven, published for all eternity. You may live unnoticed now, but one day God himself will publicly, before all the hosts of heaven, declare you to be his crowning jewel. Oh, glory!

I (Nan) am a library hound. There's no place I love to be more than a library. So the idea of there being one in heaven makes me glad I'm going there all the more. I love to browse the biography section, looking for books about people who led courageous lives. I read about them and am inspired to live my life in a way that will have great impact.

We can easily picture it: The volumes in heaven are filling even now with accounts of our faithfulness. One day you'll browse the rows of books and you'll come across a volume containing the account of your days. It will tell of your faithful acts of doing the laundry, dishes washed, car-pools driven with love and tenderness. You'll read of the moment you took the hand of a discouraged friend and said, "Don't give up. God will be faithful." You'll stare in amazement as you read of the times you changed a diaper, cleaned up vomit, and wiped a feverish forehead and said those nightly prayers for your angry teen-ager and encouraged her to believe God. You'll be shocked to see that he noticed all the times you bit your tongue when you wanted to lash out at a rude coworker.

Don't doubt it for a moment, dear daughter. You may be thinking, *My life sure won't make very exciting reading.* Well, maybe not to you. But God has recorded it because it delights him. He takes note of it all and is waiting eagerly to reward you for every bit of it. What? Rewards for a diaper change? Don't take my word for it.

Let's go to Hebrews 11:6.

What two things are true about the person who pleases God?

1.

2.

God is not only looking for those who believe he exists. (Most people believe that. So do the demons.) He also is looking for those who believe he is a rewarder! No good thing you say or do escapes his loving gaze. His books are full of your acts of obedience and the vaults of heaven are full of treasures marked out for you. So take joy in those cups of cold water given in the form of an encouraging word or a loving admonition to your child.

Read Psalm 130:3-4.

What did God not keep a record of that made David so happy?

_____

_____

According to Romans 4:3-8, what is God keeping a record of?

_____

_____

Praise be to our God for remembering our best moments and forgetting our less exemplary episodes. We stand on a level playing field in the eyes of God. We are his beloved daughters! Miriam is remembered in biblical history for sibling heroism. This brave heroine is smiled upon for her fierce courage in the face of overwhelming odds. God's presence and will for her life played out over many years. Like all of us, she had her own share of messy moments and lapses in judgment. But her shining moment came as a teen-age first child commissioned to step up and do what was necessary to protect her youngest brother. How fun it will be to check out her book in heaven's library: *The Biography of a Fearless Sister,* published by God.

Take some time to imagine the reunion back home. Jochebed watching the banks of the river, praying for both her eldest and youngest child, heart pounding, waiting for any sign of their return. What news would Miriam bring? Would Miriam carry the burden of guilt if her brother had been killed? Would Jochebed be able to console her daughter while grieving the loss of her son? What if Miriam had been taken from the river? What if she had been raped or worse?

Here's a fun exercise for you and your study partner. One of you is Jochebed, the other is Miriam carrying her brother home. Write down what you would have said to each other.

_____

_____

_____

_____

We would love to join you in this! Here's what we imagined:

Jochebed sees Miriam coming through the water carrying the basket. Miriam is laughing out loud. Jochebed rushes into the water, and can barely breathe by the time she holds her daughter and son in her arms. They are covered with mud, soaked head to toe and talking at the same time.

J: Is he...?

M: Momma, you won't believe it! Yes! Look, he's fine! (Miriam pulls back the cover of the ark and there is Moses, needing a diaper change, but thrilled to see his mother. Jochebed picks up her baby son and inhales the feel of his body. He giggles and then immediately begins a hungry search for her breast.)

J: Come, let's get out of this river and into some dry clothes. Tell me everything! (Mother and daughter carry Moses out of the Nile and onto the river banks. They collapse with joy.)

M: Momma, Momma, the princess wants take care of him!

J: So they were bathing?

M: Yes, Momma, just like you hoped.

J: Praise God! Praise God! What happened?

M: I think I did good, Momma. I think it's all going to be good.

(And the rest is history.)

The words of David, a song for the dedication of the Temple, might have summed up the joy of this family reunion.

Read Psalm 30:10-12.

Truly the Lord showed mercy. He was their helper and deliverer.

Jochebed and Miriam might have been planning a funeral. Instead, the baby Moses was nursing at his mother's breast and his sister saved the day! Surely they praised Jehovah for his great power and their laughter must have filled the air.

TODAY'S DATE: _____

YOUR HEADLINE:

_____

Your God watches over your children. It's not for you or me to understand the currents of the river, or the unlikely people God will use to shape their lives. Be encouraged again today by the intertwining stories of these three women. Our God is the drama king!

BREAKING NEWS

World News

RUMORS OF PRINCESS ADOPTION STUN PALACE

Some Say He is Son of Sargon

Mystery continues to shroud the news of a tiny son, secretly adopted by Pharaoh's daughter. Court officials refuse to answer details surrounding the child's birth. Everyone knows the princess to be childless and no one has come forward to describe her pregnancy.

The high level of secrecy has stirred rumors that the child may be the Son of Sargon.

Historians are openly debating the possibilities. We know from ancient prophecy a male child will be born to a high priestess with an unknown father. His name will be Sargon of Accad and he will become a great ruler in central Mesopotamia. Accordingly, Sargon's birth will be kept secret. It is said his mother will set him in the bulrushes, where the baby king will be drawn out from the water.

If our current princess is indeed the priestess of Egyptian prophecy, then her son will bring much favor to our land. The fabled Son of Sargon will one day gain the love of Ishtar, goddess of love and war. It is Ishtar who will grant Sargon title to the throne. [5]

Rumors from palace sources have been few and quickly hushed. But bizarre reports are surfacing. Unnamed sources have seen the princess, holding secret meetings with a family of unknown origin at her private bathhouse on the Nile River.

Stranger still is the unknown identity of the child's wet nurse.

All in all, this adds up to more questions than answers from a royal family well known for holding their cards close to their chest.

World News offers a handsome reward to any credible information about this newly adopted son of Pharaoh.

The King's heart is in the hand of the Lord, as are the watercourses:
He turns it whichever way He wills. Prov. 21:1 Amplified Bible

TODAY'S HEROINE:
The Princess of Egypt

Read Exodus 2:5-10.

It's one thing to read of the wild faith of the midwives and Jochebed. For Christ-following women, we can close our eyes and try to imagine being Miriam, wading through the river-banks, watching her brother float toward an unknown future. We love to tell the stories of these brave "fore-sisters" of the Word. God used them, blessed them, saved them, and delivered them.

It's not so easy to comprehend how God uses the women who did not call him Lord. Yet the pages of Scripture are filled with just as many stories of deliverance falling on the ungodly as on the righteous. Why would an Egyptian princess have the honor of raising Moses? Why would she draw him out of the water and bring him up in the tradition of idol worship?

At the climactic moment when Miriam watches the Princess of Egypt with her brother's tiny ark, what are her thoughts? It's difficult to imagine that Jochebed and Miriam had not discussed this very scene. Egyptians believed the Nile River gave them special powers, blessing, covering. Moses' basket was sent in the direction of the enemy. Miriam, watching along the shore, must have caught her breath when indeed, the basket was pulled from the Nile by a princess's royal hands.

It's not too much of a stretch to hear the intake of Miriam's breath as the princess opens the basket and looks at the Hebrew child. Will the princess throw him in the water to drown? Time must have slowed in motion as she watched for the reaction of the women bathing with the princess. Her heart pounds. Then she breathes a sigh of relief as the royal pool party begins to smile and coo at him. The princess uncovers the baby and he begins to cry. Miriam can see the princess is touched by his beauty. So she seizes the moment and steps out of hiding.

Mercy lines up next to injustice over and over again.

Without explanation, without our approval, God's grace falls on those he uses for his kingdom purposes.

Read Daniel 2:21.

How does this verse apply to Pharaoh's daughter and the fate of the baby Moses?

_____

_____

_____

By offering to find a wet nurse, Miriam is helping the princess along toward a decision to keep the baby alive. The princess does not seem to hesitate at all. On the spur of the moment, she agrees to defy her father's edict of murder. She takes a step of courage and secretly finances the care and feeding of a Hebrew baby boy. She hires Jochebed, and pays her from the royal treasury to nurse her own child. Pharaoh's money was being used to keep a male

Hebrew baby well fed. Surely God has a divine sense of humor!

The Lord can use anyone, even people who don't have a clue who he is and don't care about his laws. He can and does turn the hearts of powerful people to make decisions that accomplish his will. Modern politics often leave us frustrated and fearful for the future. We take comfort in knowing our God sets people in power and removes people from power.

Break down our opening verse from Proverbs 21:1 (Amplified Bible):

"The _____ _____ is in the hand of the Lord, as are the _____:

He _____ it _____ _____ ___ wills."

He is not asleep at the wheel of eternity, nor was he then when the Egyptian princess would preserve the life of Moses, adopting him as her own son. Our God is sovereign.

Now turn to Acts 7:21-22.

Describe the relationship between the princess and her adopted child.

_____

_____

_____

_____

_____

We love the simple, profound description used in the NIV. Acts 7:20 reads, "At that time Moses was born, and he was no ordinary child." No kidding! And he had no ordinary childhood. The princess "rescued him and took him and reared him as her own son" (Amplified Bible).

How could Jochebed have imagined that the very hands of the king's daughter, the very place demanding the death of newborn babies, would be the hands of a patroness, offering life and a future?

Delight in the following providential tag-team ballet of grace: .

From Jochebed's arms, from Miriam's watchful eyes, to the arms of the enemy's daughter. Then from the princess to Miriam back to Jochebed's nursing breast. Arms of a mother, hands of a sister, arms of a princess, then back around again.

In this interchange we see God honoring Jochebed's faith through the kindness of an Egyptian princess. We're guessing there must have been some kind of official document explaining Moses' adoption. Maybe there was an off-the-record, wink-and-nod deal permitting the baby's off-site visits to his parents' home. It's intriguing to wonder how Jochebed was given permission to nurse the child. What bittersweet joy for his family to love him in those early years, whispering to him of his heritage as a chosen man of God.

Imagine your words to your son, had you been in her situation. You would have told him of his roots and where he came from and the family he was leaving behind. You wouldn't have been able to teach him about God the way you had planned. So you would pray for him to know God as Jehovah, supreme above any earthly gods he would encounter in the courts of Egypt.

Jochebed had her son back, but only for a short time. She would have known that once he was weaned, he would leave her arms forever. How she must have savored every moment with him. Gazing into his eyes as he nursed, watching him take his first steps and say, "Momma." She must have prayed fervently.

What would Moses understand by the official hand-off time from Jochebed to the royal court? If he was weaned at age two or three, and then suddenly taken from his mother, all he could grasp would be the pain of abandonment. We cannot imagine Jochebed's pain in knowing she must let him go. It reminds us of Hannah when she left Samuel at the temple with Eli. At least Hannah knew her son would be raised to know the living God. Jochebed was releasing her son into a wicked and pagan culture to be raised by an idol worshiper. What sustained her mother's heart? How did she find any peace in all of this? She must have known the character of God. She must have been anchored in his faithfulness and goodness. How else could she have survived?

In light of baby Moses, read the familiar promises of Jeremiah 29:11-14.

If the Lord were speaking this over the heart of Jochebed regarding Moses' future, what would she know?

_____

_____

_____

_____

_____

Jehovah God specializes in drawing his people out from the most unthinkable slavery, the most unlikely situations, and back to his heart. He allows the clock to tick on his timetable. And when the time comes, he will be found.

This extraordinary Moses child indeed had the best of both worlds. Nursed by his birth mother, he was then cared for by the most powerful woman in the world. The Egyptian court would groom him for the throne. (At the time of his "adoption," Pharaoh had no male heir. The princess would have raised Moses to be king.)

Acts 7:22 packs a loaded sentence.

"Educated in the wisdom and culture of the Egyptian… he was mighty (powerful) in his speech and deeds (Amplified Bible).

The court curriculum would most likely have included political science, public administration, religion, history, geometry and perhaps even engineering and hydraulics. [4] (Makes us wonder if this didn't all come in rather handy when he was put in charge of a wandering nation crossing a desert to an unknown land.) Pharaoh's princess may have seen his education as preparation for Egypt's rule. God used it for a much grander purpose: the making of a strong deliverer.

Nelson's New Illustrated Biblical Commentary has an observation of Moses' life we find fascinating:

"It has been said that Moses spent forty years thinking he was somebody, then spent forty years finding out he was nobody. Finally, he spent forty years finding out what God could do with somebody who was nobody." [5]

When Jochebed's baby boy is returned to the palace, he is a nobody graced with the royal title of a somebody. The princess has given him a special name: Moses, or "he who draws out." We wonder what Jochecbed thought of this name. We like to imagine she took comfort in the meaning. It meant one thing to the princess, but something entirely different to Jochebed. Did she pray that her boy would know he was drawn out because he was a Hebrew? Did she hope with all her heart that though surrounded by idols and false gods he would one day choose to set himself apart and worship the one true living God?

Yes, Jehovah! Draw Moses out! Set him apart for You! Keep his heart free from false gods! Jochebed's prayers sound like yours and ours. We want our children to know God above the noise and clamor of our culture. We pray for their lives to follow his path, his calling. We hit the floor, face down pleading their case, trusting God to do the work he promised. We ask the Holy Spirit to hover over them and birth truth. We praise Jesus for being everpresent as their Savior.

Thankfully we don't have to build a floating cradle and hide our babies in bulrushes to save their lives. God did the eternal suffering, took the biggest risk, and allows us the unspeakable grace of choice. Yet in a figurative sense, how can we build a boat of faith for our children to sail? In the daily care of all God has entrusted to you, how do we protect and guard their lives?

Again we find ourselves wrestling with the process of trust and letting go.

Everything we've been given must be given back to God. In the letting go, we launch our treasures and offer them back. Like Jochebed, we give God our hearts, our children. Like Miriam we stand, watch and wait to speak out on their behalf, no matter the danger. And even women like the princess find enough grit to buck the world system and choose to protect the most helpless among us, especially our children.

Jochebed's prayers were answered. God drew Moses out to deliver the entire Hebrew nation. Through Moses, God drew them out of slavery into freedom.

The midwives, Jochebed, Miriam and the Princess of Egypt went out of their way to take care of this baby boy. There's something about a baby that brings out a primal nurturing instinct in a woman. These women used their wisdom and drew on reserves of courage to take action in a dangerous situation. They were alert to the situation as it unfolded and made their decisions each day weighing the risk.

From women who dared to do each next right thing, a young baby's life was saved and

God's perfect will was carried out to perfection. There's no way to comprehend God's ways. Yet it is endlessly encouraging to watch the flesh and blood women of history playing out their roles to his glory.

From every direction. From those who bowed their knee to Sargon and Egyptian monuments, to those who trusted in the promises passed down from Jacob to Joseph. From midwives who understood the priceless intentionality of a human baby's life, from mothers and sisters who bucked the system, to a princess who turned a palace into an orphanage.

Our God is able to deliver. He will use kings and powers of rulers, princes, and princesses for His sovereign will and purposes. Like the waters he spoke into existence, speaking land to be separate from seas, he guides the waters of the human heart.

Pause now and fill in today's date and your personal headline.

TODAY'S DATE: _____

YOUR HEADLINE:

_____

If the waters of your heart are raging with worry, let them be calmed by the knowledge that your God understands. If you know Jesus, remember he spoke to storms and dangerous currents and peace fell at his command. The Holy Spirit runs through it and is the ultimate gift to you and me, in the shallow and the deep.

Recall how God uses those who are in power to have his mercy unfold. No one can go too far, or be too close to drowning, that his arms don't extend farther. Who knows? Perhaps this Egyptian princess was eternally changed. God is the only one who can take a kernel of courage and turn it into a mountain of faith.

The Bronze-Age BEACON

1405 B. C.   End of Late Bronze Age [6]

Citizens Of Ai Put On Highest Terror Alert

Conditions in Ai: Highest Terror Alert. Israelite nation headed this direction.

Pollution Index: High levels of smoke from west wind carrying debris from the burning, fallen city of Jericho.

Ai's city officials have been closely monitoring events as the Israelite nation marched quietly around Jericho over the past week. On day seven came the horrendous sounds of horns blowing and the unexplainable collapse of her walls. Our city's close proximity to Jericho has put Ai on high alert. Be prepared to leave at any moment.

Red Light District Dame from Jericho May Be Armed, Dangerous

ALL-POINTS BULLETIN: Information is sought concerning the whereabouts of one of Jericho's most infamous and powerful CEOs, the owner of Rahab Inc. Unnamed sources say they have reason to believe Rahab is the ringleader of this terrorist attack on the city of Jericho. She and her family are the only suspected survivors. They are missing and presumed to be on the run. An all-out military effort is underway to find the owner of this successful escort service.

Some wonder if the primary stockholder of Rahab Inc. has mysteriously disappeared into the ranks of the Hebrew nation. For years, Jericho's government officials, perhaps too tightly wound in the web of disclosure, refused public demands from their citizens to shut her down. The company's website may well have listed a clientele that would have embarrassed many of Jericho's most powerful citizens.

Ai's military met this morning to begin a search party for Ms. Rahab. If she is captured and talks, perhaps Ai can be spared an attack from this rogue nation. Curiously, the house of Rahab still stands on the short stretch of the north side of Jericho's wall. This portion of mudbrick wall still remains to a height of over eight feet! [7]

Top CSI experts have been sent from Ai's security offices this morning to look for clues. Early reports confirm Rahab's computer files were destroyed. Unexplainable is a ragged strand of dark red linen taken from under the pile of rocks near her empty home.

Rest assured, Ai will not go quietly into the hands of this blustering Israelite nation. It will take more than shouting and the sound of the shofar to win a battle over our great city. The name Ai means "ruin" and "heap," which is exactly what we plan to make of these Hebrews: a ruined heap!

On a lighter note, to honor the losses of Jericho, Ai plans a special time of Baal worship at sundown. We'll be taking donations and offering sacrifices in an effort to keep the gods on our side.

For the sake of Jacob, My servant, and of Israel My chosen, I have called you by your name… though you have not known Me. I am the Lord, and there is no one else; there is no God besides Me. I will gird and arm you, though you have not known Me.
Isa. 45:4-5 Amplified Bible

TODAY'S HEROINE:
Rahab, former harlot, presently the great-great-grandmother of King David

If you haven't met her before, you will now meet the most famous of all the "ladies of the night." Rahab was a practicing member of the world's oldest profession. The scarlet cord that saved her life regrettably inspired the term associated with a "red light" in the window: the massage parlor is open. You're about to discover the true salvation story behind this famous red cord.

How could a slut, whore, harlot be a biblical heroine?

How could Rahab be listed in Matthew 1, only one of four women who are named in the genealogy of Jesus?

How could she be lauded and honored in the Hebrews 11 Hall of Faith?

What mighty works did she do that would earn such accolades?

Get this: Rahab simply believed God.

Her story is a riveting reminder of how much faith means to our God. It delights his heart. He never wastes even a seemingly wasted life that awakens to his call.

Turn to Ephesians 1:4.

Who chooses those who will come to faith in God?

_____

When were we chosen?

_____

In whom are we found?

_____

God credits righteousness to a prostitute who knew nothing of him but what she had heard through the grapevine. What she heard of God convinced her to believe in him as the only God. Her faith was used to save her life, the lives of Israel's spies, the lives of her family, and her soul. Her faith in God deposited Rahab into her true destiny in the line of God's son. All because she believed.

As we arrive to study Rahab's adventure, we have fast-tracked past Moses and the deliverance of Israel from Egypt. We are now in the book of Joshua with this new leader of God's people. During their years in the wilderness, God moved mightily to protect, discipline, teach, move, and guide his nation. Now they are ready to inhabit the land of his promise.

In the opening chapters of Joshua, the people of God are near the city of Jericho. The people of Jericho knew they were there. The guards patrolling the walls had been watching them for some time. The Hebrews had camped two miles away, just across the Jordan River. As the people of Jericho trembled and watched to see what these worshipers of Yahweh would do, they recounted stories of the amazing things this God had done for them in Egypt.

So what are they doing here? they must have wondered. *What are they planning?* The people of Jericho did not know the Hebrews were waiting for a report from two spies sent into their city. They waited on eyewitness reports about the lay of the land. Then they would cross the river and silently march forward, beginning the process of claiming the land God has promised to be their inheritance forever.

Read Deuteronomy 9 and describe the foreshadowing of what will happen in Jericho.

_____

_____

_____

But why send spies into a city God has already promised to give? The Hebrews did not know it, but inside those city walls was a woman with a tiny mustard seed of faith. One of God's chosen who believed in him would be used to deliver his spies and to find deliverance for herself and her family from the coming invasion. What the Hebrews could not have comprehended would be that Rahab would be this beloved woman of faith. A harlot who made her career in the world's oldest profession would be joining the Hebrew nation and become part of their history.

Turn now to Joshua 6:19-21 to read God's specific commands for the defeat of Jericho.

Do you find any of this disturbing? If so, explain.

_____

_____

_____

When we read about the destruction of Jericho, it's difficult to imagine God's instructions to destroy all the people, young and old. But this wasn't the first time God called for complete destruction. In Noah's time, the entire world was so evil God was grieved and moved to destroy everything except Noah, his family, and the animals.

It also was true with Sodom and Gomorrah in the book of Genesis. It's almost unthinkable that these cities were so corrupt that the men would come out at night to demand sex with visitors. They were so given over to depravity that only Lot and his family, for a time, kept God's wrath at bay. Like Sodom and Gomorrah, Jericho was a city filled with every kind of evil, with one family to be spared: Rahab and her household. God's great pain over the wickedness of the world always is overcome by his redemptive love.

In 1405 B.C., from six to seven acres in size, Jericho was the oldest city in the world. Its inhabitants worshiped the moon, and for the previous 500 years had fallen into moral decline. By the time God told the Israelites to take the city and destroy its inhabitants, the citizens of Jericho were practicing child sacrifice, sodomy, and religious as well as secular prostitution.

The city was nestled in the Jordan Valley and was heavily fortified by a double wall. (This double wall may have given the inhabitants a sense of invincibility. It also makes God's powerful collapse of the city without a single battle being fought even more breathtakingly glorious!)

The poorest people of the town lived in the space between the upper and lower walls. This was not prime real estate and certainly would not have been safe in a time of war. If a battle was to occur, the walls would be the first place of attack. Some of these houses were connected to the lower wall. The back wall of their rooms was inside the lower wall. Their roofs were the top of the wall.

Living in the lower wall of this godless, idol-worshiping town was Rahab. We have no record of her having a husband. Possibly she was a widow. She was most likely very poor and may have chosen prostitution as her only means of survival.

One commentary suggests the following description of our brave heroine:

"Rahab was a common prostitute, not the word for cultic prostitute. It is possible that Rahab had been reduced to prostitution by the death of her husband and by the needs of her impoverished family. In any case, out of all the populace of Jericho, only she reached out to the living God, and he in turn saved her."[8]

Her dwelling in the wall was humble. On the poor side of town, in the projects. It had a window and a flat roof which she used to lay out her flax and dry it in the sun. From the flax she would have made linen for clothing. Stalks of flax, perfect for hiding spies. A window perfect for an escape and rescue mission.

It's time to visit the riveting second chapter of Joshua. But take your time; don't miss one verse.

What is your favorite part of her story?

_____

_____

_____

How did she describe the mood of Jericho in **verse 11**?

_____

_____

Everyone in Jericho had heard of Jehovah, but Rahab alone chose to believe in the God of the Israelites. Along with everyone else in the region, she had heard the stories of the powerful Yahweh who had dried up the Red Sea and led his children out of Egypt. They knew how God had given the Israelites victory over the attacking Amorites and how the Hebrews had defeated them and captured their cities. In a city terrified of this God, Rahab's fear had turned to faith.

Read Exodus 15:13-16.

As the children of Israel made their way through the desert to Canaan, breaking news was making its way to the surrounding nations. What effect did the name of Jehovah cause?

_____

_____

Is this not thrilling? The fame of God had spread. His name began wearing away at the walls of the Canaanites' minds long before the walls of the city came down.

Rahab meditated on the stories of the slave nation delivered out of bondage and set free from the cruelest, mightiest nation on earth. This must have resonated with her own bondage. Did she feel like a prisoner too? A slave to the choices she had made with life? Was prostitution paying her bills but robbing her soul? Rahab was attracted to the stories of hopeless people being given a second chance at life. As we read of her bold courage in helping the spies, it's easy to hear her voice calling out to believe in this God of mercy, believing he would deliver her as well.

As with the midwives in Exodus, we find another woman facing imminent threats from her government. Without looking back to Exodus 1, try to write down a few similarities between Egypt's midwives and Rahab.

_____

_____

_____

_____

Yes, once again we find a woman caught in a political quagmire, faced with trusting God over government.

Once more, faith in God wins out over fear of man.

Let's look at how Rahab walked out faith with each step she took with the two spies. This story reads like the best suspense novel, and as with all great mysteries, we are left with unanswered questions.

How did the spies from Israel know how to find the house of a harlot in a strange city? Why did they trust her? One explanation has to make any woman smile a bit. "They went to a place where news would be easily available, a prostitute's house." [9]Who else would know the scoop on just about everyone and everything in town but someone who had visits from men representing every political and economic bracket?

God alone knows the details.

We do know Joshua sent out two scouts. And somewhere locked away in Joshua 2:1 are the answers to why these spies were quickly knocking on the door of a prostitute's flop house.

Then talk about news traveling fast in a small town! How in the world did the king of Jericho know the Israeli spies were spotted at Rahab's house? Was she already being watched by authorities? Maybe one of the king's men was leaving Rahab after his usual visit and noticed some strangers in town headed her way. We'll have to line up in heaven, along with many others, to visit Rahab's new house and find the answers.

Regardless of how she made a living, Rahab emerges as a radical, brilliant businesswoman. One could easily build a case for her being one of the Bible's first God-honoring feminists. This lady was sharp. Quick on her feet when threatened, and precise in conversation.

Imagine the rush of adrenaline as she heard a knock at her door.

What decisive action had Rahab taken in **verse 6?**

_____

_____

Israel's spies were lying under stalks of flax as she rushed to answer the king's policemen. Rahab's lie was bold and clear. That's not to make a case for lying. But she moved to protect God's men. She did the best she could and perhaps defaulted to lying as a means for her own survival.

Can you think of a time or place when you would lie to save someone out of respect for God?

_____

_____

_____

God hates lying. But he also looks at the heart. **Read 1 John 3:20** and relate this verse to Rahab's life, profession and choices in lying about the spies.

_____

_____

_____

Eugene Peterson's *The Message* puts it this way: **"God is greater than our worried**

hearts and knows more about us than we do ourselves."

This unlikely daughter of God was used to hide his special agents. Only God could orchestrate such events that would save so many and preserve an inheritance that would lead to the birth of his son!

Let's look at Joshua 2:9-14 and take apart her confession to the spies.

What had Jericho heard about God?

_____

_____

Did Rahab include herself in their reaction?

_____

_____

To what conclusion did Rahab come after hearing this news?

_____

_____

What did she boldly request of the spies?

_____

_____

Rahab literally confirmed God's prophetic words about the Promised Land. She tells the spies she knows the Lord has given them the land, and her use of the name "Yahweh" shows she has come to faith in him!

Several sources try to paint Rahab's response to the spies as one of pure self protection. Maybe it's too much of a stretch for some to believe a prostitute could be saved and used of God. One of the strangest interpretations attributed her conversation with the spies as a motivation to tell them what they "wanted to hear" to save her neck.

The pages of Scripture don't reveal any such description. When Rahab hid the spies and lied, she sided with Israel against her own people—an act of treason! Her testimony, amazingly from this pagan lost woman, evidenced one of the most powerful conversions in biblical history. She already had decided that Jehovah was her God, not the gods worshiped in her culture. And Rahab was willing to risk everything to save the Hebrew spies.

After cleverly sending Jericho's guards in the wrong direction in hot pursuit of Israel's spies, Rahab made her heart's desire crystal clear. Like one of Israel's finest historians, she recited the deeds of the Lord, and her use of his name says it all: LORD. In Scripture, LORD in capital letters refers to the covenantal Lord, the LORD who promised on his name to Abram in Genesis 15:18 to stand by his Word. Rahab was one informed lady, spiritually in tune with God's heart.

In Joshua 2:11, Rahab turns the corner from bondage to freedom. Write in your own words her confession of faith.

_____

_____

_____

"For the Lord your God is God in heaven above and on the earth below" (NIV). In an act of great boldness she reaches out for salvation without an altar call. Not only does she want to be physically saved from the oncoming destruction, but she also wants this God for her own. It seems as if she says, "I want what you have inherited. I want to know this God who is all powerful and protects his people."

To the credit of the spies, they don't deny her. They don't say, "No, sorry. We can't share him with anyone who is not Hebrew." They offer her what God offered them: the covering of blood.

Read Joshua 2:17-21.

What did the spies tell Rahab to do?

_____

_____

What was her response?

_____

Instead of blood on the doorposts, they tell her to hang a scarlet cord in her window. In Egypt when the death angel came, the blood covered God's people and delivered them. When death approached the people of Jericho, the scarlet cord would spare both Rahab and her family. The blood on the doorposts and the scarlet cord in the window were a foreshadowing of the blood of Jesus on the cross.

As she let down the scarlet cord from the window of her house in Jericho, so God pre-ordained the scarlet cord of blood to cover her house, in real time and in his time. There's no way to read Rahab's story and not run headlong into the cross of Jesus.

Turn to Exodus 12:13.

What scarlet promise do we find for our heroine?

_____

_____

Now, a sidebar for discussion.

Rahab and the spies had put God's plan into motion. She helped them escape over the wall by letting them down from her window by a rope. They would look for a scarlet cord to fall from this same window to save her household when the city fell. (Her house was probably on the north side of the city wall. Her window would have faced the badlands of the Judean wilderness, where she told the spies to hide in the hills for three days before returning to camp. This also is the area Jesus referred to in the parable of the Good Samaritan on the dangerous road to Jericho.) [9]

Use your sanctified imagination for a moment here.

When the spies safely escaped and reported back to Joshua, what would have been the response from the Hebrews that a prostitute was coming their way for safe haven? As a woman, can you imagine how this information might have been huge fodder for outrage and indignation?

"God uses anyone for his glory," might be one response. "Are you kidding? Prostitutes are to be stoned!" another. "The spies stayed with them." Silence. "I'm just saying, that's a little weird, don't you think? A hooker's house?" "Did you say her name was Rahab the harlot? Did I hear that right?"

Or, better yet, the wives of the spies at home that night.

"Tell me, please tell me, there is somewhere else you could have gone! And don't tell me you went there because she made the best couscous in town!"

What would you have said to your best friend about Rahab?

_____

_____

_____

Sometimes it's hard for us to accept the people God chooses. Why is that? Perhaps it's because we've lost sight of how deeply we all need grace. If we think our sins are not as bad as someone else's, then we have opened the door to pride and self-righteousness. That's a scary place we don't want to go. It was the self-righteous, religious people of his day that made Jesus furious. We don't want him to turn our way and say, "Woe to you, self-righteous hypocrites!"

Read Matthew 21:28-32.

Why was Jesus angry?

_____

_____

What kind of people was He teaching that day?

_____

_____

Who will enter the kingdom of God ahead of others?

_____

_____

Why?

_____

_____

Sometimes when my (Nan's) big extended family gets together for a meal, we'll begin to talk about our ancestors. Some have gone down in our lore in a rather one-dimensional way. They are remembered by one or two qualities or character flaws, and we'll tell and retell a particular story in which they are featured as the buffoon. "Remember Aunt So-And-So with the acid tongue who could really level you with a few choice words? She was never really nice to me."

Or:

"Remember great uncle What's-His-Name with the eyebrow hairs long enough to braid?"

Or:

"Great Grandmother What's-it? The one with the really big hair? Remember how her dentures clicked when she talked?"

We can be tacky!

On a deeper level, we give people lifelong labels for things they have done even though long ago they were forgiven. We see a couple at church and think to ourselves, "There's the guy who was unfaithful to his wife," instead of seeing him as the one who repented and was reconciled and is now walking in faithfulness. Or perhaps it's the divorced woman or the child born out of wedlock that we are unable to see without those labels.

We wonder at how we remember Rahab. We grew up hearing her called nothing but "Rahab the harlot." Well, she didn't stay a harlot. She left that way of life and became a member of the family of God. She came to faith in a living God and was totally transformed. But do we now remember her as, "Rahab the ancestor of Jesus?" No, we still call her "Rahab the harlot." Maybe it's because that's how she's described in the book of Joshua (Josh. 6:25 Amplified Bible), and even referred to by this title when he calls for her family to be spared.

Still somehow it seems unfair. If God doesn't look at her that way, why should we? We just can't seem to let things go and see people as God sees all of us. When we are in Christ Jesus, we are righteous in God's eyes. He looks at us with love and sees his pure and spotless bride.

Can we not do the same for each other?

When the Israelites recalled their stories to one another in the generations to come, we can imagine them talking about Rahab in glowing terms. They would say she was the one who sheltered the spies. She was the one who opened the door to the first military victory in the Promised Land. She was the courageous lady who dared to believe that Yahweh was the one true God even though she had never before been a part of the covenant people.

There would have been no need to bring up her former career.

In heaven, when we get to meet Rahab, we hope we have the courtesy not to refer to her in any other terms but the ones that show her a new creation, as well as one of our heroines! We can see it now. Someone will introduce us to her and we'll stutter and stammer, "Oh, yes, we read all about you! You're Rahab the... the... great-great-grandmother of Jesus! So pleased to meet you!"

Is there someone you need to find new eyes to see?

Write their initials here and say a prayer for God's vision of who they are in him:

_____

We give labels but God sees potential. He never leaves us where we are, but keeps shaping and refining us till we look just like his son. It's time to celebrate who people are, not what they aren't, or used to be. If God had seen Rahab only as a harlot, there would have been no hope for her.

Has there been a time in your past when you felt there was no hope? A label you wore like a scarlet letter?

In Matthew 1:5 we read of a man named Salmon who became the husband of Rahab. What it was like when Rahab and her family joined the Israelites after Jericho was conquered? The Hebrew nation must have accepted and honored her for the vital role she played in their victory. And Salmon chose to help her put the past behind her by asking her to be his wife. This man Salmon was a prince and the head of the tribe of Judah.

God honored Rahab again by giving her a son named Boaz!

We know this good man from the book of Ruth. He was the kinsman-redeemer of Naomi who married a Moabite woman named Ruth. Boaz saw a worthy woman in need and helped her even though she was considered an outsider and apart from the blessings of God. You see, Boaz had experience with this kind of thing. His own mother had once been an outsider named Rahab the harlot.

Do you see the scarlet thread as it weaves through biblical history, full of grace, mercy, redemption, forgiveness and hope? If this historical lineage is new to you, please take a moment and write about how this makes you feel.

_____

_____

_____

Boaz knew the story of what happened to his momma before he was born. She was born outside the covenant of God but was chosen by him and used to help the people of Israel. He married Ruth, and by this act he identified himself with our own kinsman-redeemer, the Lord Jesus Christ, who came to save people from all nations, tongues, and tribes. God rewarded the faithfulness of Boaz, who one day became the great-grandfather of King David.

What a beautiful tapestry we behold as we follow the scarlet cord.

Salmon, Rahab, Boaz, and Ruth are pictures of our God of grace reaching out to the person standing outside the covenant. In this way, God aligns himself with the helpless. These women who stood on the outside were taken in and allowed to participate in the lineage of Jesus!

Amazing!

Rahab, an Amorite woman, became the great-great-grandmother of King David.

What a glorious and merciful God we adore. There is none like him. Not because we are worthy does he choose us, but simply as a display of his everlasting love.

Thank God he doesn't limit his sight to what we are at any given moment. He sees what we are becoming. We need to give each other the same grace God so freely lavishes on us. We need to pray for others to have the classic reversal of destiny that God longs to give those who do not yet know him.

Remember the spies are not named in this story, but Rahab is. Once again, when writing the history of the Jews, Moses included the name of a woman.

Rahab, we can't wait to knock on your door!

Bless you, Lord, for Rahab's story, and for your grace. Thank you that even in the crevice of a wall in a doomed city, you find your girl!

Now, back to our story.

Rahab had heard of the Passover events in Egypt. Her city trembled in their boots when Jehovah's name came up at the dinner table. "EL," as they called God, had wiped out the first-born of Egypt in one night. EL was a force to be reckoned with and not taken lightly. Rahab now immersed herself in the story of EL's promise.

EL was on the move. Jericho was in danger. Rahab did not flinch in the face of this challenge. She rose up and claimed EL to be her God. And as disturbing as it may appear, she did not ask the spies to hand out scarlet cords for her friends, her neighbors, or her book club. Rahab clearly wanted protection over her family and agreed to keep the plan secret.

> One scarlet cord would fall.
> One city would fall.
> One legacy would be redeemed.
> One lamb would be born.

Rahab's story teaches us not to write off or consider anyone past hope. Who are we to say someone cannot change? Her life is a huge reminder to all of us that God knows where we are, who we are, what to do to call us, and what we are capable of doing.

Did she lay awake at night and dream of being a heroine who would be used in the extraordinary warfare of God's people? This harlot, living in a wall, would have been voted "Least Likely to Succeed" by her graduating class. Yet she saw God as her deliverer.

Did she dream of being swept away by a knight on a white horse? Little did she know her heart's readiness to receive God would place her name in the coveted line that would birth the king of kings. And when Jesus her savior returns, he will come back on a white horse with his church by his side, Rahab smiling ear to ear. Surely she could not have dreamed of such a glorious destiny. But then, God delights in turning the most desperate situation into a display of his stunning mercy.

So this messy, tough woman of the world tied a scarlet cord in her window and tied her heart to Israel's blood of the covenant. Her story will forever be linked to their history. No other nation, before or since, has had the covenantal covering and overcoming spirit of the nation of Israel. Three thousand years later we are still telling their story and right smack in the earliest books one cannot skip over Rahab the harlot.

We look to the blood of the cross of Jesus, through which all nations are invited to be his. Rahab reminds us that he knows exactly who will come, who to save, who to call and who to use.

Unlikely or not, Rahab and her family were grafted in to the bloodline of God's covering. Perhaps for the first time in her life, she didn't have to work or carry the responsibility of earning favor. Perhaps for the first time she could hold her head up high and relax in the shadow of God's wings.

All she had to do was align herself with him and believe.

Reread today's opening verse from Isaiah 45:4-5.

What might Rahab have written in her private journal to this declaration that God would choose her, even though she had not known him?

_____

_____

God not only chose her for salvation. He also chose her along with Tamar, Ruth, and Bath-sheba to be great-grandmothers of the Lord Jesus Christ. God chooses those with faith to partner with him in his plan for redemption. There is no one so far gone into sin that God cannot save them and use them for his glorious purposes.

Her story reminds us that God knows where we are, even if we're walled up in a godless culture, doing unspeakable things to make it through the day and night. God knows if our hearts will hear his voice and come to him, to new life.

If you ever feel your faith is not enough to please God, remember Rahab.

If you ever feel your works will make him love you more, remember Rahab's job description.

Her faith was huge. Her works were outrageous. She lied, hid God's beloved, and asked without hesitation for a "Get-Out-of-Jericho-Free" card for herself and her family.

By any human standard, Rahab would fall into the following categories:

LOSER
LOW LIFE
LOST
LEFT BEHIND

And yet, in God's book, she is remembered:

BELOVED
EMBRACED
GRACED
HONORABLE
WALKING THE RED CARPET OF DELIVERANCE!

"Too late" is not found in Rahab's biography. "To be continued?" Absolutely.

Read Joshua 6:25 for the end of her beginning.

Now fill in today's date and your headline.

TODAY'S DATE: _____

YOUR HEADLINE:

_____

Who have you given up on? What do you pray for them in the light of Rahab's story?

Oh yes, beloved girlfriend, believe God! Believe he works in the strangest, unknowable of all ways.

Believe in the scarlet cord of the blood of his son!

"There are four ways God answers prayers. No, not yet. No, I love you too much. Yes, I thought you'd never ask. Yes, and here's more."

God's answer to Rahab's story: "Here's more!"

News&Notes

FAMILY OF JUDAH ROCKED BY SCANDAL
Who Let the Twins Out?

Genesis 38: Read it and weep.

For decades rumors have swirled about the head of Judah, the well known son of Jacob, Israel's patriarch. It started years ago with suspicious claims of Judah's participation in the disappearance of his youngest brother, Joseph. The story grows more suspicious as we learn that he broke ranks with his Hebrew brothers by choosing to live with an unnamed Canaanite woman, an anonymous daughter of Shuah. Their romance proved strong. During their time together, three sons were born.

Oddly, only one survived.

No one knows exactly why each son died or disappeared, leaving only one daughter-in-law, Tamar, to fend for herself. And so the plot thickens.

By Hittite law, the widow of a brother who dies is by right entitled to marry his brother. [10] Tamar believed her father-in-law to be following this guarantee when he promised her marriage to an unnamed future heir.

But without making good on his legal obligations to Tamar, and without warning, Judah disappeared into the highlands. His staff refused to elaborate, except to offer a vague reference to his involvement with the annual sheep-shearing guild meeting.

Tamar was not a happy camper.

After learning of his flight from town, she waited for his return.

Anonymous reports cite Judah as a frequent visitor to our local brothels. Sources who refuse to go on record insist they watched Tamar, dressed as a goddess harlot, waiting for her father-in-law to pass by his usual stomping grounds.

Without going into the sordid details, News and Notes reporters have learned that Judah was seduced by his daughter-in-law, who got away with more than just his credit cards and personal identification. Posing as a prostitute, Tamar cleverly hid her appearance behind one of the latest fashion trends. Like most men, Judah was no match for a veiled, pretty face.

Soon after their encounter, before a judge and jury could line up for a juicy trial, Judah and Tamar settled matters out of court.

"She has been more righteous and just than I, because I did not live up to

my word," said Judah at a public hearing. *"I will not see her or do her injustice in the future."*

However, no good deed goes unpunished.

Today Tamar gave birth to twin sons. None will name the father, but she claims their heritage to fall under the covering of Judah's God. Her sons, Zerah and Perez, made quite an entrance.

The midwife reports:

"When the first boy's hand came out, I put a scarlet thread on him. Then he pulled back his hand and out came his brother! It was quite a day for everyone!"

What a breaking forth you have made for yourself! Gen. 38:29 Amplified Bible

TODAY'S HEROINE:
Tamar, daughter-in-law of Judah

A strange chapter is tucked into the middle of Joseph's story in the book of Genesis. It happens right after Joseph's brothers sell him into slavery. For some reason, Moses (the author) stops the narrative here to insert Genesis 38, a huge chapter in the life of Judah.

Morally speaking, this was not a shining time for the sons of Israel. In a previous chapter, Simeon and Levi murder the entire male population of Shechem and carry off all the women, children, and wealth of the city as plunder. A little later, Reuben sleeps with his father's concubine, Bilhah. Then when the youngest brother Joseph gets on their one last nerve, the brothers sell him into slavery and lie to their father, saying Joseph was killed by a wild beast. These men don't seem likely candidates for the lineage of the coming messiah.

In Genesis 38, we find Judah leaving home and traveling to Canaan. Maybe he left the family homestead because he couldn't bear the guilt he felt over his part in selling Joseph. Maybe he was unable to deal with the look on Jacob, his grieving father's face. For whatever reason, Judah left and moved to Canaan, where he married a Gentile woman. Strange choice, leaving one family nightmare to create another. To marry an idol-worshiping Canaanite was against the will of God. Hebrews were to marry Hebrews. The fact that Judah was comfortable with marrying a Gentile shows how little he esteemed the commands of God, and how easily he blended into the pagan culture of the day.

Over the next few years, Judah's wife Bath-shua gave birth to three boys. Judah's firstborn was named Er, and as soon as he was old enough, Judah found a wife for him. This woman too was a Canaanite. Her name was Tamar.

It's interesting to recall God's original plan. He asked the men of Israel to stay clear of Canaanite women. Yet boys will be boys. And some of these Canaanite ladies became God's very testimony, his heroines. The fierce faith of the women—women like Tamar—won them favor in his eyes. In our twenty-first century, the Internet is an endless source of information that offers us a peek into ancient cultures. There are random and specific facts, speculative dot-coms, and everything in between. A "Google-ing" of the name "Tamar" reveals everything from biblical references to recording artists. Her name left a mark on history, and it's been used from Genesis to the present day as a provocative title.

Tamar's name (emphasis on the first syllable) means "a palm tree."[10]

Indeed, as we read her story we see a woman who stood strong as a tree against the fierce winds of injustice. She was mistreated by her father-in-law, Judah, but she would not go quietly without putting up a fight.

The name of Tamar still calls out today, demanding to be heard. If we listen closely enough, her voice can be heard in the cry of every God-fearing woman who has been abused and tossed aside. Hers is the story of a desperate widow who went to extreme measures in order to put herself in God's path.

As with Jacob, Tamar wrestled for an answer, and demanded God's blessing. Faith isn't always a pretty picture. Her story tears at the core of a woman's heart. Yet like Rahab, she infuses our hearts with her courage.

Turn to Genesis 38:1-6.

What were the names of Judah's sons?

_____

_____

According to **verses 6-11**, what choices was Tamar allowed to make concerning the direction of her life?

_____

_____

To whom was Tamar married?

_____

By **verse 11**, what had happened to Tamar and her husbands?

_____

_____

Tamar's husband Er was a wicked man. The Scripture says that because of his wickedness, God put him to death. This happened early in their marriage, before any children were born. Judah then told his second son, Onan, to have children by his sister-in-law so that his dead brother's name would live on. Onan used birth control to prevent Tamar from getting pregnant. This, too, was wicked in God's sight, so down went another son, struck dead because of disobedience.

What might have been written on their tombstones?

_____

_____

Perhaps: "Here lie brothers Er and Onan. They displeased the Lord and he slew them." Quite a sobering legacy.

In his anguish over losing two sons, Judah tells Tamar to go home. He sends her back to Canaan and tells her to live as a widow.

Yet what one last promise did Judah make?

_____

_____

While keeping his fingers crossed behind his back, Judah promises that her widowhood will be temporary, just until his youngest son is grown. Then Tamar will be his wife when he's of age. But Judah has no intention of keeping his word. He believes Tamar is bad luck and wouldn't dream of giving his youngest son a death sentence by marrying him off to her.

What does his line of rationalization reveal? It shows how blind Judah was to the sinful ways of his own sons. He blamed their deaths not on their disobedience to God, but on Tamar, the victim of their disobedience.

How often do we want to blame someone else for our own actions?

Now more time goes by. Judah's wife dies. His youngest son grows into manhood. Still Tamar's phone doesn't ring. Her hopes fade as she realizes that Judah has no intention to honor the ancient tradition of a levirate marriage.

"In the ancient Near East, for a man to die without leaving a son was regarded as an incalculable loss. A person's memory was preserved in his descendants. In order to maintain the family line and the name of the deceased, a brother or another near relative would marry the man's widow and father a child that would carry on the man's family. This is called a levirate marriage, from a Latin word meaning 'husband's brother.'"[11]

Tamar counted on this levirate marriage, the Hebrew law, and the word of her father-in-law, Judah. She had witnessed the blessings of Judah's family. She was a Canaanite, but she based her every hope in the God of Judah's legacy.

Yet year after year continued to pass. Tamar was dismissed by Judah and left to fend for herself. So what's a girl to do? In her culture, what were Tamar's options?

Write the first four words of **verse 12**: _____ __ _____ _____

In many translations, they are "after a long time." That speaks volumes, doesn't it? Remaining a widow in her father's house meant a future with no children, and a life with no purpose. So after much consideration, perhaps anguish, disgusted at her own thought processes, Tamar decided to take drastic measures to stay in Judah's covenant family.

And now, a sidebar. For all their moral failures, there was something about the sons of Israel that was much more appealing to this Canaanite girl than the thought of living out the rest of her days with idol worshipers. What attracted Tamar to this wildly dysfunctional crew? Marriage to Er was no cakewalk. Yet we find this Gentile woman drawn to their faith in a God who blessed, and a God who was alive and full of mercy. What is it about Tamar's story that applies to you and me? It's so hard to imagine this kind of desperation for a spiritual inheritance. If in her place, would most of us opt for widowhood?

Let's think about our own moments of desperation for Jesus.

Can you relate to wanting to be a Christ-follower despite the behavior of some in the church?

_____

_____

Tamar certainly would have much to say to all of us on this matter.

As her story continues, we see she was nobody's fool. She watched and waited, and came up with a startling plan to get back into the family of the promise.

Judah knew it was time to make good on his word. So he skipped town. When it came down to keeping his promises, Judah headed for the hills of Timnah. The time of sheep shearing was not only a time of working; it also was a time of celebration. Judah was partying down while Tamar waited at home.

Another phrase in **verse 13** tells us that Tamar was definitely out of the loop. What four words begin this passage? In the NIV translation, it reads, "When Tamar was told." She may have heard it through the grapevine, but Tamar had her ear to the ground. Without a husband, with no hope for her future, the time had come. She decided to beat Judah at his own game. She knew his weak spots; she knew her power. Nothing would stop her from finding her place as God's woman.

Tamar's actions appear to be outrageous. She wants a child of the promise. She wants to be part of this family line. She devises a plan that makes us cringe at the very thought of it. Yet listen to the following description of her situation.

"Her desperate act was driven by a sense of injustice. On the one hand, Judah had broken his promise to marry her to Shelah. On the other hand, she had done nothing to deserve becoming a forgotten widow; her husband's deaths were not her fault." [12]

Over and again the Lord makes very clear his feelings about the orphaned and widowed. He commands that they be taken care of and treated with respect and care. Here we find that Judah's repeated lies and dismissive attitude toward Tamar result in bringing him to shame. Like Rahab, Tamar made her way into the lineage that would birth Jesus. In God's economy, faith covers a multitude of failures.

So, Judah would leave town. Fine. No problem. Tamar would wait until he came home. She knew her father-in-law all too well.

According to **verses 13-16**, what did Tamar know of Judah's character?

_____

_____

Knowing Judah as she does, she knows how to attract his attention. Tamar dresses like a temple prostitute with a veil hiding her face. And she waits.

Temple prostitutes were at the top of the food chain. They were not like the common streetwalker. Your average hooker in those days walked around openly displaying her face, attempting to be as physically alluring as possible. The temple girls, however, veiled their faces so the act of sexual intercourse would seem less physical and resemble an act of "worship," offered to the idol of one's choice. This was what Judah preferred. Tamar knew he felt a little less guilty about his promiscuity, since sex with a temple prostitute wasn't quite as sexy as the other kind. Cultic (also known as "sacred") prostitutes brought in the highest dollar. The veils maintained a strange fiction. This sexual tryst would be a "spiritual" negotiation.

Quite the negotiators! Quite the negotiations! Seems like Judah met his match in Tamar. With skill and clever maneuvering, she managed to conceal her identity, mask her voice, and deceive her father-in-law. Judah chose a sacred prostitute, a woman tied directly to the goddess, Asherah. Rowing farther down the river of denial, these harlots also were thought to be "virgins," over and over and over again. [13]

Did Tamar know of Judah's visits to this intersection in the road? One has to believe she was well aware of her father-in-law's visits to the sacred ladies of the night.

In **verses 16-18**, we find the terms of negotiation for her service.

What did Tamar ask of Judah?

_____

_____

She managed to talk Judah into giving her his signet ring, signet cord, and staff. In essence he gave her his credit card, his identity, his seal of authority. These items would later come back to haunt him, but save her life and the lives of the sons borne from their encounter.

Tamar waits for him to walk by and solicit her business. Sure enough, right on cue, Judah walks into the scene and falls for the trap. She is in the middle of her monthly cycle and the timing is perfect. Tamar becomes pregnant by her father-in-law.

After their not-so-spiritual tryst, Tamar quickly returned home and slipped back into the garments of her widowhood. These clothes were a constant reminder of Judah's broken promises to the community.

Tamar just wouldn't go away. She was persistent to follow any and every path to assure herself of a future in Judah's heritage. With God as her witness, to play with the words of Scarlett O'Hara, "if she had to lie, cheat, steal, or become pregnant with her father-in-law's children, she was never going to be forgotten again!"

What was Judah's initial reaction after their encounter in **verses 20-21?**

_____

_____

Something wasn't right. Maybe she seemed, dare he think, too familiar? And she had his credit cards! His conscience must have burned with a desire to find out her identity and have her put away.

Three months later when Tamar began to look pregnant, she was accused of prostitution.

In **verse 24**, what did Judah think was the proper response to a woman pregnant out of wedlock?

_____

_____

Why such harsh judgment on his daughter-in-law? What overriding emotion moved him to such anger?

_____

_____

Guilt. Guilt without the mercy of God brings on nothing but shame, despair, and irrational reactions. Three months had passed and his annoyance levels grew. Gossip spread about Tamar playing the harlot. When Judah heard this, he was quick to call for her execution. "Aha! Now I can lawfully get rid of this woman!" What an expedient way to release him from any obligation to give her in marriage to his youngest son. Thinking he was about to be rid of her once and for all, Judah demanded Tamar be brought forth and burned.

The irony and hypocrisy of his outrage was short lived. Judah, one of the heirs of God's everlasting covenant, would not be put to shame by a Canaanite woman. In contrast, the very woman he brought into his household would be used of God to bring him to his knees.

Verse 25 is packed with high drama. Tamar must have been waiting for this very moment. She stood tall, looked Judah in the eye, and made public the identity of the man whose child she would bear. The buck stopped with Judah.

Describe Tamar's declaration in your own words:

_____

_____

"Make out clearly, I pray you, to whom these belong" (Amplified Bible). And out came the ring, the cord, and staff. A courtroom trial attorney couldn't have offered a more powerful closing argument.

To his credit, Judah must have had a moment of remembering who he was, to whom he belonged. He was a man of God's covenant and he had grossly mistreated this daughter of his family.

Read verse 26. What adjective did Judah use to describe Tamar?

_____

Righteous. More righteous is this Canaanite woman than was the man of the tribe of Israel. Confession is good for the soul. Judah owned his sins, and publicly offered her grace and protection. His response was sincere and humble.

According to Hebrew law, what could have happened to both of them?

Find an answer in Leviticus 18:15-29.

_____

_____

Then there is Leviticus 20:12.

_____

_____

_____

In **Genesis 38: 26**, we learn that Judah "did not sleep with her again" (NIV). This implies that Tamar was brought back into the family and lived as part of the tribe of Judah. It implies that Judah remembered the Levitical law in his heritage and applied this to his daughter-in-law. How relieved Tamar must have been!

Read the final verses 27-30.

Six months later, Tamar was blessed by God with the birth of twin boys. The birth of two sons was considered a special blessing from the Lord. Enter another midwife! (Did you ever realize how important the midwives were in biblical history?)

Playing the classic game of "me first," they were pushing and shoving each other even in the womb. Their birthing was not easy. Zerah pushed his arm out first. The midwife tied a scarlet thread on his wrist to proclaim him the firstborn.

What did the midwife say in response?

_____

_____

"What a breaking forth you have made for yourself!" (Amplified Bible) By saying this, the midwife named him Perez, which means "breaking forth." Soon after, his elder brother decided to follow his lead. Zerah arrived, scarlet thread on his hand, his name meaning "scarlet."

From Tamar's insistent pursuit of God, from observing the covering of Jehovah's people, from her heart's desire to have a future with the Lord, two sons were born into the line of David.

Read Matthew 1:3. Who is listed as the mother of twin boys?

_____

This little boy Perez is listed as the son of Tamar and an ancestor of the Lord Jesus Christ. A child born of incest, an ancestor of Jesus!

Some people today feel that children conceived from rape or incest should be aborted. What hope could this story give to a woman facing such a decision?

_____

_____

_____

What does **Jeremiah 29:11** say about the plans God has for each of his children?

_____

_____

_____

This promise was given to his people while in captivity in Babylon! Not on a sunny day when life was easy, but in the hardest of times.

According to **Jeremiah 1:5**, how long has God known each of us?

_____

_____

God's inclusion of pagan people in the genealogy of Jesus is a picture of his gracious inclusion of all nations in the plan of salvation. Certainly Tamar and Judah's behavior is nothing we would want to emulate. But their story shows the mercy of God on all sinners. It's a living color revelation that nothing and no one can derail the plans of God. None are too wicked that they cannot be used by him to accomplish his ultimate purposes. No circumstance is too trashy, too sordid, that God won't get involved and redeem. God takes the worst satan can throw at a person and proclaims his right to turn that circumstance around to his glory and for the good of his children.

Tamar lived in a totally different culture. She saw no other way out. A childless woman in our time is not confined to a purposeless life of misery. For Tamar, she wanted her part in the heritage of the children of Israel so much she was literally willing to sell herself to get it.

We don't work for our salvation. It's not something we earn. We certainly don't have to debase ourselves to become a part of the body of Christ. If we learn anything from Tamar, it's that we don't earn our inheritance in Christ. In God's mercy, he chose us, grafted us into this lineage, and made us joint heirs with his son Jesus. We have a place in his family, a gift Jesus paid for and we could never deserve.

We know this because we live on the side of the cross that looks back to see how the story unfolds. From long ago, when animal sacrifices were used for atonement of sin to the perfect blood sacrifice of Jesus, we are able to see the miraculous love of God.

Tamar only had her experience in Israel's family. As a young girl growing up a Gentile, she had witnessed the savagery of idol worship. She must have tasted and found the Lord Yahweh to be good, and would settle for nothing less than having a bloodline in him. We are united to Tamar in this way. We know what it's like to walk in fellowship with Jesus. We who have made him Lord know what close communion with our maker feels like, how it fills the voids and brings joy. We also know the misery that comes when we choose to walk in sin. Once you've tasted the sweetness of walking with Jesus, you can never disobey him again without the need for repentance that brings contentment.

Like Tamar, there's nothing on this earth worth the price of losing our place with God, our intimacy with Jesus, our place in his loving arms. Perhaps we relate most to her as someone who regularly heard the stories of Yahweh and his promises. Like any who know him, we hunger as a deer pants for water to be in his presence.

Turn now to 1 Chronicles 2:3-8 and read "the rest of the story!"

Both Zerah and Perez would one day have established families in the house of Judah. The legacy of Tamar lived on in Jewish history long after she was gone. When Jewish elders wanted to pronounce a blessing on Ruth and Boaz, they invoked the name of Tamar.

"Through the offspring the Lord gives you by this young woman, may your family be like that of Perez, whom Tamar bore to Judah" (Ruth 4:12, NIV).

It's thrilling to see God's intentional mercy toward Tamar, the redemption of her life, and the gift of two sons from the most unlikely scenario! Today's heroine, Tamar, overcame her heritage, overcame her actions, and emerges as a woman of great honor.

Tamar will forever be a woman transformed by the grace of God.

Now write today's date and your own headline. Make it your own.

TODAY'S DATE: _____

YOUR HEADLINE:

_____

To what lengths are you willing to go for God's blessing and favor? He waits for all of us to be fools for his love. You can't go so far that he isn't there, watching, loving every desperate grasp for his hand. And the scarlet thread of his son's blood runs in every direction.

Break forth, beloved, and receive!

Hebrew Gazette

IF THESE WALLS COULD SPEAK

Early this morning, screams were heard coming from the halls of the palace, through the windows of King David's daughter's room. Tamar was sighted tearing her richly colored robes and openly shrieking, completely undone. Until today, our beautiful young princess wore the robes of a virgin. If reports prove true, then her wailing suggests foul play, even rape.

What's going on in the king's house? It's the kind of obscenity found in a sordid novel, and unfortunately more and more the kind of behavior we find coming from our king's family.

Jonadab, the cocky cousin of the royal family, was overheard bragging about a plan he had concocted with Tamar's half-brother Amnon. However, as he was about to elaborate on the details, King David's personal guards pulled him aside and a private tongue lashing ensued.

No one inside the palace gates would speak to the press. When asked about the emotional state of the princess, we were told there would be no official comment from the king.

Any news about Tamar can be anonymously reported to the *Gazette* and would be highly appreciated. We also are curious about the drastic weight loss program of her brother Amnon.

He who justifies the wicked and he who condemns the righteous are both an abomination (exceedingly disgusting and hateful) to the Lord. Prov. 17:15 Amplified Bible

TODAY'S HEROINE:
Tamar, daughter of King David

Today's heroine is a beloved daughter of God, another woman named Tamar. She is most difficult to study. Perhaps it's because many of us share her wounds, or because someone close to us has suffered a fate like hers.

She's a heroine because she represents every sexual abuse victim who has ever lived.

Her tragedy blazes from the pages of Scripture to remind us of how God hates sexual abuse and any lies perpetrated to cover up and further humiliate the innocent victim of such a violent act.

Sometimes the injustice, unfairness, and cruelty of life can be overwhelming. It can so demoralize people that they are left desolate for the rest of their lives. A victim of violent abuse often spends a lifetime in recovery. It's especially hard to heal when they have been given the message that what happened should be minimized, kept secret, never brought into the light, or never taken to heart.

We have Tamar to thank for keeping a light shining on the atrocities of the abused. God will not cover up, nor leave out of his Word, even the ugliest torments perpetrated on the weak. He is extremely interested and takes personally what happens to his girls. There's no doubt where God stands on this issue, and on the consequences of those who attempt to escape judgment.

Sexual abuse has been described as "stealing the soul."

Let us respectfully, carefully examine the life of Tamar, the daughter of King David. Lest you are tempted to skip over Tamar's story, we urge you to be aware of how prevalent rape is in our culture. Under-reported rape continues to rob many a precious soul.

Recently I (Bonnie) accepted an invitation to meet a group of business women at a tea party in downtown Nashville. It was a sunny day, and a lovely place for new girlfriends to become acquainted. Every lady at the table was a successful writer, author, speaker, songwriter, or artist. But forget talking about business. It was the common ground of womanhood that started our conversations. We were all talking at the same time about our children and our husbands, commenting on "girl stuff" on all sides.

The beautiful new friend beside me began to talk about the nightmare of her ongoing divorce. She was midway through the process and a mother of two young sons. In an effort to make her feel encouraged, I shot out the question, "How many of us at this table have been through a divorce?" Every hand but one shot up. Sad statistics.

Someone else asked, "How many have been raped?" Every hand but two shot up. Sadder statistics still.

The only woman who had not been divorced admitted to a horrible rape, pregnancy, and regret over a resulting abortion. No one ever told her how much shame, guilt and devastation she would work to overcome. She also was the only woman out of the twelve of us who was childless. The table fell silent for a moment of honored suffering. Every one of us seemed a bit stunned by our shared sisterhood of broken places.

Nothing in me wants to ponder David's daughter Tamar. Her very existence in Scripture pushes hard into my private history. It's with the utmost humility and prayers for God's covering that I share with you my own story of sexual abuse.

In my first book, *Blessed Are the Desperate,* there's a chapter titled "Conversation with the Devil." The pages that follow describe one of the worst nights of my life. In the book I call this a "near-date-rape" experience. Ten-plus years later, I must drop the denial of the "near" defense. It was a date rape.

I'm one of many Christian women who find themselves in the single mother/divorced category. Like many others, I stumbled my way through the fog of lost dreams and into the world of dating again. In my effort to find a man who would love my children and me, I took several steps forward and a few back. Engagements came and went. Finally I took my pastor's wise advice and stopped "dating as a mission field."

I immersed myself in God's Word, prayer, loving my time with the Lord and at last, trusting him to paint the portrait of my future. I was closer to God during this time than I'd been in my entire life. Ironically, that's when the conversation with the devil began.

My children attended a wonderful private Christian school. Naively, I assumed every other parent who had a child in that school was like me. We all were trying hard to follow after God, praying that our children were traveling in the same direction. It was at this school that I met a single father of two children near the same ages as mine. After more than six weeks of small talk at school functions, even sitting next to the headmaster, the single father asked me out. I assumed this was God's provision in my life of a wonderful, godly man to date.

To cut to the literal chase, I agreed to let him pick me up at my house to take me to dinner. When he arrived, he literally walked in my front door and began to attack me. Way too much time passed as I tried to push him away. Finally I came to terms with my futile attempts to reason with the devil. I wanted so much for this man to be the person I'd been talking with on the school campus. Frankly, I should have immediately called 911 and had him arrested.

From the book, I wrote: "That night turned into a battle—with me begging to go to dinner, with him trying over and over to get me into compromising physical positions." [14] I cried; I begged. He pushed, groped, and assaulted. I tried to reason with him, which went nowhere until I threatened a lawsuit. (He was a lawyer so this seemed to hit a nerve.) He gave up and left saying, "You really must be who you say you are." But he left such damage behind.

I was shattered… confused… guilty… destroyed… sobbing… undone.

My pastor began the restoration process by turning me toward God's healing grace. My close friends scolded me with loving but strong words about how I should have called them. I recalled how Jesus was attacked by the devil in the wilderness immediately after he was baptized. But Christ didn't engage the devil in a conversation. Jesus quoted Scripture and walked away. His example is a huge one to follow for any single woman caught in this horrendous type of scenario. Don't try to reason with the enemy. Call for help. Get the guy out of your life. Get away and into safety.

When I first began public speaking, I shared this story with 400 women at a conference, and as I talked, the room became deathly quiet. I remember thinking I had crossed a line, and that no one else present had made the same dumb mistakes I had made. But the first two girls who lined up to speak with me afterward were both weeping. Both had been date raped. The second girl had become pregnant and chose to keep the baby. They were grateful for my candidness. No one in a church setting had ever addressed date rape.

Statistics from 2007 tell us that there were 248,300 victims of sexual assault that year alone. One in six women and one in thirty-three men will be sexually assaulted in their lifetime. College-age women are four times more likely to be assaulted. Every two minutes someone in the United States becomes a victim of abuse. [15]

In **2 Samuel 13**, God gives compassion, honor, and voice to every woman who has lived through such abuse. The story of Tamar is included in Scripture for many reasons. It also tells another chapter in the life of David, the king of Israel.

At this time in his reign, the horrible consequences of his sin with Bathsheba are unfolding. The sword, violence, and death are unwelcome yet permanent guests in his kingdom and family.

David had many wives. Along with these marriages came much pain and heartbreaking consequences. Tamar and her brother Absalom were children of David's wife, Maacah.

Let's turn with care to read the story of Tamar in 2 Samuel 13.

In **verses 1-2**, how was Tamar related to Amnon?

_____

How was Tamar described?

_____

_____

Amnon and Tamar had different mothers. (By the way, this was never God's plan for marriage. His plan is found in Genesis 2: One man, one woman, unashamed, and delighting in each other.) In the opening of 2 Samuel 13, we read about the horror of this blended royal family.

Read on: Verses 2-4.

Why was Amnon losing weight?

_____

_____

Quite an obsessive young man. On the brink of losing utter control, he makes matters worse by getting counsel from the wrong dude.

Describe the advice from "clever" cousin Jonadab in **verse 5.**

_____

_____

Lie to your dad, the king.

Lie to Tamar.

Move in for the thrill. You can have whatever you want, just gotta want it badly enough. Brick by brick, lie by lie, deceitful plan by deceitful heart, the groundwork is laid for destruction.

Our unsuspecting heroine is lured into her brother's living quarters by her own father's request: "Go to the house of your brother Amnon and prepare some food for him" (NIV).

When I (Nan) was growing up, I often asked my parents if I could go somewhere or do a particular thing. My parents would size up the situation and make their judgments accordingly. Sometimes they said no to me simply because where I wanted to be or who I would be with created a situation that might look inappropriate or even be dangerous. When I protested, they were quick to say that they trusted me to behave myself, but the "look" of the situation was highly questionable. It made me mad at the time, but looking back, I can see why they were concerned. My daughters soon will be approaching the age when they will be in college, out with friends and away from my supervision. Tamar's heartbreaking story is a wake-up call for me. I want to teach my girls to run from any situation that doesn't look respectful for a godly young lady. Appearances can be deceiving, but appearances also are important. Reputations are worth protecting. I pray my daughters will want to conduct themselves in a pure and holy manner. As their Momma, I will continue to tell them to run from any place that might be compromising or put them in danger.

In stark contrast, Tamar was encouraged **by her parent** to walk into a dangerous, highly suspect situation. Why was she sent to Amnon's house and into his bedroom unescorted? Even if Amnon had been an honorable man, it would not look honorable for her to be in his bedroom. To use a good old-fashioned Southern phrase, "It was improper!"

David may have been a man who sought God with all his heart. But in these chapters he walks out one of the most damaging, heinous episodes of his life. David was a lousy father when his daughter needed him most. Women were not treated fairly in his time, but this goes into the territory of mental, physical, and emotional cruelty.

As unthinkable as it seems, not only does Amnon set a trap for Tamar, but he also elicits his father's help in the plan. What does Amnon specifically request David to ask of his daughter?

Find the answer in verse 6.

_____

_____

_____

He wants her to make cakes in front of him, so that he could eat them directly from her hands!

Read on through verse 8. Imagine for a moment what this process would entail. Tamar doesn't have a microwave, or "poppin' fresh" dough. She would have to bring in the cooking utensils and prepare the cakes from scratch, kneading the dough with her lovely hands. All the while her love-sick, lust-filled half-brother would be undressing her with his eyes, planning just when and how to make his move on his unsuspecting sister.

Is there a time when you've felt extremely vulnerable or uncomfortable around a man at work? Or, worse still, perhaps even in a church setting?

_____

_____

In verse 9, read Amnon's response to Tamar's hard work.

_____

_____

What did he demand in **verse 10**?

_____

Now read verses 11-14, the rape of Tamar.

In the story of Judah, our Tamar from Genesis received an apology, a public declaration of her innocence, and a humbling response from her abuser. Here we find the daughter of David received the exact opposite treatment. She received no sympathy, only more torment.

After Amnon had his cake and his sister too, what was his reaction in **verse 15**?

_____

_____

_____

Does your heart break with mine reading her pleas in **verse 16**?

Her life was ruined. She would never marry because she had been raped.

She would never be able to hold up her head, or look another man in the face. Shamed by her brother, she was as good as dead, with any prospect of marriage or family ruined.

How did Amnon further humiliate his sister in **verse 17**?

_____

_____

"Get this woman out of here and bolt the door after her" (NIV). In essence, he used language one would use for dumping out trash.

Reading on, we see the helpless downward spiral of our heroine in **verses 18-20.**

This from the Wisconsin Coalition Against Sexual Assault: *"The incest victim is usually the healthiest in the family: the one closest to the truth and the first to seek help."*[16]

Tamar is a victim of rape as well as a victim of enforced silence. Her first response after the rape is to go public. She tears her clothes, puts dust on her head and walks around wailing for all to hear. **This is healthy. She is letting people know what has happened to her and wants something done about it.** She attempts to stand up for herself, hoping that at least some of the men in her life will defend her honor. Tamar is looking for rescue, hoping someone will fight for what she has lost.

But not even those closest to her will help. They are more concerned with their own reputations. They stifle her pain, and in doing so, stifle her very soul.

What did Absalom say to calm Tamar? **Read verse 20.**

_____

_____

"Do not tell anyone!" There it is again: Rape and abuse are supposed to be covered up, kept quiet, and gotten over. "Do not speak! Do nothing and just let everyone calm down!"

Do you think Tamar was at all comforted by his reminder that her own brother had raped her?

Family secrets are a breeding ground for despair. Sometimes people feel they must be loyal to family members, and that telling the truth about what is happening will somehow destroy the family unit. Nothing could be further from the truth. By keeping sin in the dark, there can be no healing. By bringing it into the light, redemption and freedom from guilt can bring hope to a broken heart.

Victims of abuse are defined by shame if they are not allowed to tell the truth and receive help. Tamar was told by her brother Absalom to not "take this thing to heart" (NIV). Yeah, right. Where was she supposed to take this harrowing experience? To her father who suggested she go to Amnon's room in the first place? Was there another woman in the house? We don't find a single shoulder for her to fall on. No, the ugly incident was to be swept under the family carpet. Tamar was left to bear the burden of guilt alone, unaided, unheard, unforgiven.

Again, word from the Wisconsin Coalition Against Sexual Assault: "Many abuse victims will report that the actual physical sexual abuse was not the worst aspect of the experience; rather, it was carrying such a powerful secret that must be protected." [17]

This broken, destroyed daughter is subjected to further humiliation by the response—or or non-response—from her father, King David.

Read verse 21.

What did David do?

_____

I hope you wrote, "Nothing." That's the sad truth of it. He was angry, and did nothing.

Under Mosaic Law (Lev. 20:17) Amnon deserved the death penalty. Perhaps David had a nauseating flashback to the time when lust brought him to take another man's wife, to commit murder, to lose the firstborn child of his union with Bathsheba. Amnon was next in line for the throne of Israel.

What word describes Tamar in the last part of **verse 20**?

_____

A desolate woman. The word 'desolate' was used to describe ravaged cities and ruined lands. Tamar was disgraced and unable to speak of the crime committed against her. One would assume her father, the king of Israel, would come to her defense. Like many modern-day victims, Tamar's rape would go unreported.

In the United States, more than seventy percent of all rapes go unreported.

Approximately sixty-two percent of female rape victims knew their assailant. [18]

The United States has the highest rape rate among countries which report such statistics: Four times higher than that of Germany, thirteen times higher than that of England, and twenty times higher than that of Japan.

Tamar receives no justice. She has nowhere to turn, no hope for her future.

Absalom takes her into his home, where she is hidden away. Amnon receives no punishment… at least not for two years.

Did Amnon think perhaps his firstborn rights would save his royal behind? After all, he was the son of the most famous king in Israel. Surely he'd get away with whatever he wanted. Didn't David prove this to be true? People in authority can feel they are above the law. David thought he was above the law when he took Uriah's wife Bathsheba for himself and had Uriah killed in battle. Now his son Amnon feels he is like his dad. He's above the law as well. He lusts after his half-sister, figures out how to rape her, then throws her out like a sack of trash. Amnon shows no remorse, nor is he held accountable for his actions.

Like father, like son? Not so fast.

David and Amnon were, at their core, very different men.

Lest we forget the difference between David and his son, **turn to read Psalm 51.**

What does David show us in the outpouring of his heart in the aftermath of his sin?

_____

_____

_____

Amnon never repents or asks God to forgive the sins committed first and above all against God himself. He never asks Tamar to forgive him. He never comes clean with his brothers.

Secrets kill.

Secrets killed more than just the heart of Tamar.

Read the conclusion of this horrific story in 2 Samuel 13:22-31.

Like a Greek tragedy, the senseless rape of Tamar enraged her brother Absalom. No one spoke or took action. So Absalom moved to avenge his sister's life. He killed Amnon. The saga of David's losses and grief for his family pile up, agony upon agony, until war breaks out between them. The rape of Tamar literally tore the house of David apart, son against son, son against father.

By the closing verses of 2 **Samuel 18**, we read David's cry:

"Would to God I had died for you, O Absalom, my son, my son" (Amplified Bible).

Would to God they had all walked with integrity in how they treated the lady of their house. Would to God someone had stepped forward to talk about the elephant in the king's living room! Would to God David had shown a compassionate heart toward his daughter and set his house in order.

There's no way to leave this discussion without believing if Tamar were here today, she would tell her story with eyes that understand redemption. Nothing separates us from the love of God. He was by her side during every second of the anonymous years to come. Surely Tamar would speak of God's presence in her pain. It's not hard to imagine Tamar also would plead with any abused woman to let go of any wounded secrets and receive healing, counsel, and help.

Tamar had no options. Thankfully, the modern woman does. There is help available twenty-four hours a day, seven days a week through the National Sexual Assault Hotline: 1-800-865-HOPE. There also is healing for the heart and spirit found in God's Word.

No one who has suffered sexual abuse need live as a victim. As with Tamar, a life of desolation was never God's plan for any of us. In **verse 19** we see a vivid picture of how Tamar showed her grief.

How are we allowed to grieve today?

_____

_____

Is there a heartache in your life that you have not felt permission to grieve?

_____

_____

Turn to Psalm 34:18 and read it aloud.

"The Lord is close to the brokenhearted and saves those who are crushed in spirit" (NIV).

Are you taking steps toward his healing? Or perhaps helping someone who needs such help in finding his hand to give them courage?

_____

_____

_____

God wants us to see ourselves as he sees us. Not as victims, but as beloved victors over this world. Who are we in his sight? Let's look at a few verses that tell us who we are in Christ Jesus.

In **Matthew 5:4**, what does God promise to do for you?

_____

_____

_____

According to **Luke 12:6-7**, how valuable are you in the sight of God?

_____

_____

_____

What detail does he have the exact number for?

_____

In **John 14:1-3**, what does Jesus promise to do for God's children?

_____

_____

Romans 8:28 tells us what God has promised to do with all the events of our lives, good and bad. And what is that?

_____

_____

According to 1 **Peter 2:9**, who are we?

_____

_____

_____

What can separate us from the love of God? Look in **Romans 8:35-39.**

_____

No matter what has happened to us or what we've done, God does not view us in light of our tragedies or failures. The events of our lives do not have to define us, most certainly the ones forced upon us. They do not dictate how we must live. God alone and his work on our behalf are what set us free to live beyond our pain.

Tamar's story is for all women who have been treated as though they were worthless. God wants to lift up your head, to look into your eyes, and to heal your heart. According to **Jeremiah 17:7-8**, what kind of life does God desire for you?

_____

_____

_____

Now for today's headline and date. Please fill it in as you feel led.

TODAY'S DATE: _____

YOUR HEADLINE:

_____

If there has been any intimate abuse in your life, or in the life of someone you love, please pray for them at this point in the study. Believe God to reach all of us in the places in deepest need of healing.

David's daughter Tamar is a heroine for all who have endured silent shame from unreported sexual abuse and lived without seeing a human judge bring down the gavel or place her perpetrator behind bars. But there is a judge who sees all, and knows every hair on each head. God so loves his daughters that he alone promises to have the final word about their healing. Justice will come, and it will be complete.

Jehovah God has the final word on our healing.

Turn to Isaiah 57: 15-16, 18-20 and let the Word of God fall into and over your broken places.

"God lives forever and is holy.
He is high and lifted up. He says, 'I live in a high and holy place,

but I also live with people who are sad and humble.
I give new life to those who are humble, and to those whose
hearts are broken....'

'I have seen what they have done, but I will heal them.
I will guide them and comfort them and those who felt sad for them.
They will all praise me.
I will give peace, real peace, to those far and near, and I will heal
them,'" says the Lord (New Century Version).

Praise the Lord God who takes the Tamars of this world into his arms, and gives them a place in his lap where they can cry mascara marks of pain down his royal robes. In his presence there is healing, no shame, no guilt, no fear of dreaded memories.

In his arms there is peace, and in his perfect time, lasting justice.

PEOPLE OF THE EAST

Weekly Rag

BRIDE SURPRISE ALTAR SWAP

Family Feud Settled Out of Court Stop the presses! Grab a Kleenex! We cannot make this stuff up!

JACOB AGREED: SEVEN TO FOURTEEN YEARS

As we've been reporting, one of the community's most prominent and wealthy families has been rocked with scandal. This morning, Laban of Nahor was surrounded by a team of high-powered attorneys as he left the court, hurrying away from *People of the East*'s reporters. Laban's two daughters, Leah and Rachel, also left separately from their father and each other, both still claiming their rights to be married to the same man.

The estranged sisters have been embroiled in a bizarre, lengthy legal battle over who is the rightful wife of the groom in question: a gentleman they each refer to as, "my man Jacob." Jacob was not seen at today's proceedings, most likely needing a rest from the unrelenting onslaught of media attention.

However, *People of the East* has learned that Jacob agreed to work another seven years in a settlement which will make Rachel, the youngest daughter, his bride. He is presently married to her older sister, Leah. Yes, two sisters married to the same man. There's your trouble.

It all started seven years ago on the wedding night held on Laban's private grounds. Jacob's attorney insists his client had worked on the property for seven years under a contract specifying Laban would give him the hand of the lovely Rachel. The story of Jacob and Rachel is one of love at first sight. Eyewitnesses tell of the passionate kiss between them at their first meeting by the city well. After their embrace, Jacob reportedly wept with joy.

Their man Jacob is not afraid to show his feminine side.

To sum up the complex circus of events, tables literally were overturned when Rachel and her wedding party learned that on the night of her wedding, her sister Leah had been placed under the wedding tent. Veiled in a disguise, Jacob had no idea until the next morning that he had married the elder daughter. Needless to say, it was a moonless night.

Several bridesmaids reported that all

manner of bedlam broke out the next day. "There was hair pulling and screaming and at one point I thought those two were gonna kill each other!" said Zilpah, attendant to the eldest sister, Leah.

In today's proceedings, Laban confessed he had planned the bride swap to honor our traditions of marrying the eldest daughter first. Critics are quick to note prior business deals in which Laban shrewdly deceived others, doing anything to build up his estate and power. Jacob's attorney argued vigorously that none of this was clear when Jacob entered the first seven-year agreement for Rachel, the youngest. Yet all parties appear to be relieved that a settlement has finally been reached.

Refusing to drag out the proceedings further, Jacob agreed to stay with Leah, and work another seven years to make the love of his life, Rachel, his bride. Two brides for one irate and overwhelmed groom!

There is hot talk about the family's new reality show set for next season's line up: *Life with The Laban Clan: Can't They All Just Get Along?* Should bring in terrific ratings and perhaps pay for Jacob's mounting expenses. Word is that Leah is a regular baby machine.

Because the Lord has seen my humiliation and affliction: now my husband will love me. Gen. 29:32 Amplified Bible

TODAY'S HEROINE:
Leah, a mother of many children, sister of Rachel, daughter of Laban, wife of Jacob

We often wonder why so little has been written about the complex relationship between Leah and her younger sister Rachel. Maybe that's because it had to have been extremely complicated. Few studies have tackled a close inspection of these very different sisters and their struggle with loving the same man. Once more, using our sanctified, well-informed imagination, let's sit at the feet of Scripture and meet these women on their turf.

Leah and her sister Rachel were caught in the crosshairs between their father Laban and a suitor named Jacob. Both men were masters of deceit, masking ulterior motives to achieve their own agendas. To put it bluntly, Leah and Rachel were the victims of a royal pissing contest. Father-in-law pitted against future son-in-law, both masters at manipulation and one-upmanship.

The story of these two sisters begins as we see Jacob arrive at a well in the land of Haran.

His name meant "swindler, deceiver, trickster, schemer." Jacob was the poster child for living up to a name. Posing as his younger brother, Jacob received the Abrahamic blessing from his blind, aging father, Isaac. He recently had run away from home after stealing his brother Esau's birthright. He'd been sleeping outside under the stars, using stones for a pillow. He had a dream of a ladder that reached to heaven and heard the voice of God tell him that in his seed all the families of earth would be blessed.

Pretty dramatic events so far in Jacob's young life. After waking from his dream, he makes a decision.

Read Genesis 28:12-22.

What did God promise Jacob?

_____

_____

What does Jacob promise God?

_____

_____

Jacob's promise to God is conditional. He commits to worship God as Lord only after God proves to be faithful. From Jacob's habitual deceptive behavior with his father and brother, it seems only natural that he would be slow to trust anyone, even God. Jacob certainly knew he couldn't trust himself.

Jacob was into making bargains. He bargained for Esau's birthright. He knew Esau's weakness for immediate gratification and took full advantage of his older brother. One day after Esau was famished from working all day in the fields, Jacob traded a bowl of stew for that birthright. Jacob knew that Esau would sell his very soul to fill his empty stomach. You see, Jacob excelled in waiting, watching and moving at just the right moment to get what he wanted. And so now, Jacob bargains with God, essentially saying, "If you'll do this, then I'll do that." He's not exactly a man of faith yet. The *Faith in Action Study Bible* notes that "Jacob was a 'work in progress'—another of God's salvage projects." But with the dream of the angels on the ladder ascending and descending, Jacob knows he has encountered the living God. He decided to give him a chance. Jacob set up a stone pillar (Bethel) and promised to tithe for the rest of his life if God would come through for him.

Food for thought. Can you recall moments when bargaining with God seemed logical? Have you ever played Jacob's game?

_____

_____

After receiving the blessing of God, and believing God was clear on Jacob's requirements, he is next found in Genesis 29, in the land of his uncle Laban. The well in an ancient city would have been somewhat like the Starbucks or the grocery store, Barnes & Noble, or the

YMCA in our culture. It was the place to hang out, to meet people, to catch up and swap stories, or perhaps to find romance. It also was a symbol of God's blessing and essential to life. Many significant events in Scripture happened at a well. Wells played a particularly personal role Jacob's life.

Genesis 24 records the search for Jacob's mother, Isaac's wife Rebekah. Abraham sent a trusted servant of God to find a suitable bride for his son of the promise.

Read of this astonishing adventure in Genesis 24:10-20. To what city did the servant travel?

_____

Who was Nahor?

_____

Verse 15 is packed with history. Who are the parents of Rebekah?

_____

_____

Where was Rebekah when she met Abraham's servant?

In **verse 16**, how is Rebekah described?

_____

What had Abraham's servant prayed just before she came to the well?

_____

_____

_____

Rebekah answered the prayers of Abraham's servant to the letter. He knew she was to be the woman for Isaac to marry. The servant gave her gold jewelry and adorned her with favor, implying she would be dearly taken care of by his master. A young, excited Rebekah took the servant to her home to meet her family.

Read verses 29-32. Who was Rebekah's brother?

_____

Laban immediately noticed the wealth and stature of the servant. He knew his sister was about to marry well. He took inventory of the gold jewelry and knew the favor of Abraham's family. Laban acted much like the father of the home in negotiating Rebekah's hand in marriage. (His negotiating skills grew shrewder and more cunning as the years went by.)

Jacob would have grown up hearing stories about a generous Uncle Laban who gave Rebekah his blessing. Jacob would have undoubtedly heard tales about the well and of how his lovely mother was found there by a man of God. Maybe he hoped that one day he too would have a similar divinely guided moment and meet his future bride at a well. Surely coming upon the well in Genesis 29:2 was a welcome sight for this homesick man on the run in search of his relatives.

Now let's turn our attention to Leah, Jacob's first wife.

We hope that she is going to become one of your favorite women in our study. Leah jumps off the pages of Scripture and into our lives saying, "I want a love story!" Like high school girlfriends at a sleep over, we are drawn to Leah because she represents the core dream of every woman: the desire for our own love story.

Most of us begin dreaming of love at a young age. When hormones kick in and we wake up to a world of handsome men, our dreams of true love become serious. We pray for one man, God's man, who will one day take our hand in marriage. We want him to shower us with compliments and be assured that in his eyes, we are drop-dead glorious. It's in our DNA, this desire to be loved. Leah's voice echoes our Cinderella-prayers. "Lord, please let a man come for me! Let my man love me just like I am." As we grow older the prayers are amended: "And as I age, Lord, may he be love-blind to my wrinkles, crow's feet and cellulite!"

Can we get an "Amen?"

Glancing over Leah's resume, one might assume she had it all. She had her man, children, family, and wealth. But things aren't always as they seem. We often size up certain women by their place in the social structure of the day. Leah may have come from a well-known family and been the first wife of one of the most famous men in biblical history. But look closely, and you'll find a woman who suffered humiliation, indignity, and rejection. Leah's life may have been filled with children, but her face in the family portrait reveals an ongoing sense of longing and painful questions. In the pages of Genesis 29, Leah embodies every hidden place in a woman's heart that burns with self-doubt.

Turn to Genesis 29:16-17.

Without reading further, how is Leah described?

_____

Right off the bat, without embellishment or a hint of grace we read that Leah was older and weak in the eyes! The Amplified Bible records: "Now Laban had two daughters, the name of the elder was Leah and the name of the younger was Rachel. Leah's eyes were weak and dull looking, but Rachel was beautiful and attractive." Names are important in any generation, but they held special significance in the ancient world. Since the beginning of time it has been true that physically attractive people have it easier. It's so unfair. And it hurts.

Beside Leah's high school yearbook picture, we might have read that her name meant, "wild cow." Wow; thanks a lot. (One commentary lamely suggested this description could have been a term of endearment.)[19] Can you honestly think of a single woman who would agree? Try to imagine her graduation announcement.

Laban of Nahor invites you to the graduation of his eldest daughter,

Leah, the weak, dull-eyed wild cow
First in her class, last to hear the phone ring

RSVP: Rachel, party-planner for the celebration festivities

There is no mention of Laban's wife, thus several commentaries suggest that Leah, being the oldest, would have been responsible for helping raise her younger, more attractive sister. Can you wrap your mind around the daily mental battle Leah may have faced?

An opportunity for discussion: We constantly compare ourselves to other women. Ever look in the mirror and say, "Why Lord? Why couldn't I have the _____ (fill in the blank) like _____ (her)? Lord, I know you love me. I am fearfully and wonderfully made. Couldn't you have focused a little less on the fearful part? What am I supposed to do about_____?"

Ever look around and feel like you are never going to measure up?

Well, it's time to gather around Leah and come clean about the seasons in our lives when we wanted to scream, "I will never be enough!" Our heroine, Leah, could have written a best-seller on battling female insecurity. The saga of her life as the first wife of Jacob is a textbook case of a woman trying, trying, and trying again to please a detached husband. She was supposed to be the maid of honor, not the bride. Her wedding day was the ultimate episode of *Bride Swap*.

Leah is our new girlfriend. How can we get to know her? How can we identify her hopes and dreams with ones that mirror our own?

What about this? As we turn through the pages of **Genesis 29-30**, let's imagine Leah has given us permission to read and write in her journal.

Journaling has been a part of my (Bonnie's) life since I was given my first white diary—the one with a lock and key—the one I would write in as soon as I could write. From my elementary school years until this morning, my journals have been my friend: a safe place to rant, rave, unload feelings, write bad poetry, song lyrics, and prayers. Journals keep track of life and allow one to look back and take inventory.

My journal from my sophomore year is especially tough to read. I was almost six feet tall by my freshman year of high school. I was taller than all the guys, all their fathers, and the faculty at large. Skilled in fine arts, I was greatly lacking in boyfriends. Geeky tall girls were not cool and I was surrounded by short, dimple-cheeked beauties who received the male attention I so deeply desired.

I pulled out my old diary and imagined Leah and I were reading it together. Every few lines or so it was like she nudged my elbow and said, "Exactly!" or "Me too!" or "I completely understand."

Here are few snapshots of the underbelly of my insecurity and prayers for true love.

"I cried tonight because I want to love someone so much, someone who is sweet and kind who'll treat me like a girl they love. When I see my friends and all the guys who call them it's hard not to be depressed. They have such good fortune." (Yep, I wrote "good fortune.")

"It helped my ego a lot to talk with _____. I needed some kind of boost and because of my self-consciousness of <u>being tall</u>!!! He was really sweet and polite. I pray to God he isn't lying."

My high school years were socially defined by my role as the "communications director" for my cute girlfriends and the guys who wanted the latest scoop. Desperate for attention, I took phone calls and messages back and forth, hoping one of them would look my way.

"Today was gross! First off, I looked horrible because my hair flopped. I feel so ugly and horrid. I'm going to give up on guys. I'm going to stop trying. _____ is in love with _____, _____ is in love with _____, _____is in love with _____, and everybody is in love with _____!! I am alone. I hate pity. I never ever want to fall for someone or let myself hope!"

Leah, we know you can relate.

From the vault of Leah's diaries, let's try to set the stage for the events chronicled in Genesis 29.

Write in Leah's journal: How do you imagine she felt growing up with a drop-dead gorgeous younger sister (Rachel)?

_____

_____

_____

As Jacob enters their lives, Leah has a new challenge. She must stand alone on the sidelines and watch Rachel's love story.

Read Genesis 29:1-13.

What happened to the favored younger sister? She was passionately kissed by a wealthy, well-known cousin at the town well!

Write a line or two in Leah's journal on the day Rachel met Jacob:

_____

_____

We imagine Leah would write something like this: "Once again everything went right for Rachel! Today, Rachel was swept off her feet by our cousin, Jacob. He met her at the town well and kissed her right there in front of everybody! Years ago, Jacob's mother, Aunt Rebekah, was discovered at a well. Must run in the family. His father Isaac, great-grandfather Abraham, they all seem to have the moon and stars and favor of God on their side. Now Rachel is madly in love and Jacob came to dinner tonight. Worst of all, she and Jacob were disgusting, smiling at each other all night, obviously smitten. Why not me? Why not me, God? Where is my romance story? When will my story begin?"

Now read Genesis 29:14-20.

What does Laban require of Jacob during his visit?

_____

Jacob has been staying with Laban one month when his uncle makes him a business proposition. It was customary to view women as property. Laban, ever the businessman, viewed his daughters that way. Still it feels so demeaning that, right on the heels of Laban's question to Jacob about wages, he states that he has two daughters. He must have seen the attraction between Jacob and Rachel, heard about their first embrace at the city well, and banked on driving a hard bargain for his younger daughter.

What does Jacob agree to do?

_____

Write in Leah's journal about this family transaction:

_____

_____

Here is our version:

"Sure enough, Jacob stayed like I thought he would. He's nuts about Rachel. Dad put him to work here on the grounds. This works out just peachy because Jacob and Rachel see each other every day and they are ridiculously in love. And here we go; Jacob and father have been talking about a marriage! Jacob's gonna work for seven years for her. Unbelievable!"

EDITORIAL: It's pivotal to stop and note several key points.

1. The act of choosing a bride for his son would be the father's responsibility. "Among Semitic peoples generally it is held that as the divine Father provided a wife for Adam, so the earthly father is to select a wife for his son; or in the absence of the father this duty devolves on the mother or the elder brother." [20]

Jacob negotiates directly with Laban for the hand of Rachel.

2. The act of deciding on a dowry was handled between the father of the bride and the father of the groom. Often, when a bride was chosen by the father, there would be a go-between or friend of the bridegroom who would work out the negotiations for the bride's dowry.

The reason for a dowry would be a compensation for the loss of the bride's labor in the family unit. When a family lived in a desert location, every hand was useful for making tents, weaving, and in Rachel's case, **read Genesis 29:9**. What work was she doing for Laban?

_____

"The amount of the bride price and the means (money, animals, land labor, etc.) by which it is to be paid varies from place to place.... There are certain bride prices for the different bride categories: the cousin bride, the village bride, and the stranger bride... still there must be an agreement as to the bride price in every separate case."[21]

Rachel would have been the first choice in those times, the marriage of a cousin, a princess bride. **Turn to Numbers 36:6-9.** Who did the Lord say would be best for the daughters of Zelophehad?

_____

_____

What did these marriages ensure?

_____

_____

_____

Rachel was Rebekah's niece, a beauty and a treasure. Working for her hand would have been the custom of the day. For Jacob, arriving with nothing but the clothes on his back, manual service for her father would have been a difficult dowry, but perhaps all he had to offer.

Jacob negotiated with Laban to work for seven years. Laban drove a tough bargain, but in his eyes, Jacob must have felt Rachel worth the price. **In Genesis 29:20**, how is Jacob feeling about waiting for his bride?

_____

_____

Leah, too, would have known the stories about her aunt Rebekah. Yet it's difficult to imagine that seven years would have passed so quickly for Laban's eldest daughter.

During these seven years, why didn't Laban arrange a marriage for his oldest daughter? If the father did the choosing, Leah would have been forced to wait on Laban to act. That was part of his responsibility as her father. If, as he later claims, he was all caught up in marrying the eldest daughter first, then why not take care of Leah's future first? Why didn't Laban ensure her hand during these seven years before Rachel wed? Surely Leah wondered the same thing.

This would not be the only time Laban showed little regard for the feelings of his daughters. Maybe Laban was already plotting to trick Jacob to squeeze out more time of hard labor from his nephew. Whatever wheels were spinning in Laban's mind, Leah was powerless to do anything but watch, wait and do what her father told her to do.

Imagine seven years of Leah listening to plans for Rachel's rosy future. Seven years of watching her younger sister beam with beauty and the glow that surrounds every woman preparing for marriage. Do you think Rachel was aware of Leah's loneliness? Did the two sisters giggle and wonder together about Rachel's coming wedding night? Or did Rachel have a set of younger friends to share her thoughts and laughter? For Leah, it must have been seven years of going to sleep at night with no such promises for her future, no man sighing as she passed by, no romance on the calendar.

Seven years of aging. How might seven years have further dulled Leah's weak eyes? How did seven years ripen and fill out her younger sister? Age could not have been a friend to the elder daughter. As for many single women, age may well have been the ongoing thorn in her flesh, a constant reminder that she remained unmarried with unfulfilled expectations, childless and with a few wrinkles starting to show.

Leah might have penned the following quote in her journal:

"If God had to give a woman wrinkles, He might at least have put them on the soles of her feet." [22]

At the end of seven years, Jacob has completed his work and is eager to marry Rachel. According to Middle Eastern tradition, if a public feast is given in recognition of a marriage, then the union is official and binding. Laban invites guests and prepares the celebration, which could have lasted up to seven days.

In our culture, wedding days are ripe for drama or disaster. Sweaty palms, nerves on edge, wedding planners scurrying around, hairpins flying, mothers and daughters alternately laughing, arguing, or crying. Emotions are on "stun." Family and friends gather, caught up in the enchantment of joining one man, one woman, with the fragrance of Eden in the air. Sometimes a flower girl or ring bearer steals the show, or someone forgets to bring the ring. A rain shower may pop up, or the bride might toss her bouquet to an unlikely recipient.

Our weddings can't hold a candle to the production and customs of a Middle Eastern marriage. Leah's wedding literally takes the cake. What happens next is one of the cruelest acts of deceit recorded in scripture.

Read Genesis 29:21-28.

In **Genesis 29:22,** who planned the wedding and who was gathered?

_____

_____

In Frederick Buechner's novel *The Son of Laughter*, he captures a vivid imagining of the infamous wedding. Using the voice of Jacob in first person, Buechner writes:

"I have long since forgotten the seven years, but the wedding at the end of the seventh I cannot forget. For two days the men feasted. All manner of races and dances and hand-clapping there were, the whining and mooning of pipes and windy rams' horns, the slap of goatskin drums…. Beer and date wine poured heavy as winter rain. Whole oxen were turned on spits. Wheat loaves overflowed panniers.

Laban was everywhere at once—hugging and punching, beer-breathed, sweat-stained.

The women in the meanwhile prepared the bridal tent. They spread the forked roots of mandrakes under the cushions to flame our desire though they might have known that mine, like my love, needed no flaming." [23]

Verse 23 tells us who escorted the bride "down the aisle" and to the tent:

It was Laban who fetched the bride from the house where she had been waiting with the women. He led the procession.

Here we find again Laban the control freak. The custom of the day would have been for the bride to be taken by her friends and relatives in a procession to the groom. In some instances, the groom would have gone himself to get his new bride from the house of her parents. However Laban, the manipulating father, took his daughter to Jacob's tent without allowing for any interruption.

Can you imagine the conversation between Laban and Leah when he told her what she must do? Not only was it a horrible deception and sin against Jacob and Rachel, it was totally humiliating to Leah. She was being sentenced to a loveless marriage. Was Leah forced by her father to deceive Jacob?

Another possibility is that Leah was a willing partner in the deception. Read this excerpt from commentator Warren Wiersbe to ponder another possible slant on Leah's participation in the scheme:

"Had Leah so desired, she could easily have revealed the plot, but that would have embarrassed Laban before his guests and probably led to Jacob's being banished from the home without his beloved Rachel. Then for the rest of her life, Leah would have had to live with a disappointed sister and an angry father, who would devise some means to get even with his elder daughter. No, revealing the scheme just wasn't worth it.

I feel that Leah was a willing accomplice, happy to get a hard-working husband like Jacob who would inherit Isaac's wealth and enjoy the covenant blessings of Abraham. Certainly she knew that Rachel would also be part of the bargain, but was willing to risk whatever problems might ensue. Leah may have 'borrowed' some of her sister's garments and even learned to imitate some of her personal mannerisms. If so, she was treating Jacob just the way he had treated his father when he pretended to be Esau." [24]

Another burning question revolves around the bride's preparations. A special bath would have been given her, special cosmetics, and specific layerings of dress and ornaments. Her attendants had to be complicit in the deceptive bachelorette party. During the wedding day, women would have come to sit with the bride, commenting on her appearance, complimenting the relatives, discussing family matters, eating and drinking. They would also have lit their lamps when evening fell to illuminate the path for the bride to meet her groom.

Of course, there's the nagging obvious elephant in the room: Why didn't Jacob recognize his own bride? He'd had seven years around her, for crying out loud. He might not have had permission to spend much time with her, but he walked right up and kissed her passionately at their first meeting. Some commentaries speculate that after days of free-flowing wine,

Jacob was too drunk and tired to realize he was with the wrong sister. To give him a little credit, let's look at what Leah would have been wearing.

Possible articles of dress:

1. A dress called a "queen"
2. A silk dress
3. A green dress
4. A girdle
5. An embroidered jacket of velvet or cloth
6. A black head cloth of crepe with gaily colored fringe

Ornaments

7. A chin chain
8. Bracelets
9. Finger rings [25]

To the modern mind, we wonder how Jacob could not know who he was marrying and sleeping with. In the ancient Middle East, the bride was so completely covered from head to toe in elaborate layers of fabric that she was totally hidden from the groom's sight. It's a wonder she could walk. Leah's face also may have been covered when they consummated the marriage. Obviously she must have spoken little, for Jacob was completely fooled.

"The bride came at last. I had given her a mantle stitched with linen—and she wore it over her head to show that no man except her husband would ever cover her. I waited in the dark bridal tent alone. I was half-blind with desire as well as with wine. All night I burned like a flame with the bride whom my eyes could not see through the darkness." [26]

Laban took Leah to Jacob for the wedding night and left her there to face the horror of the morning light. With the sun rising, Leah could not hide the truth. We've all heard many a sad honeymoon tale, but few compare to hers. Imagine every insecurity, every doubt of her attractiveness, every painful thought of not being enough, suddenly staring at her in the eyes of Jacob, and in his shattered, disappointed, outraged cry. "Behold, it was Leah!" (Amplified Bible) No matter what happened between them in the dark of the wedding night, the burning words of Jacob would have confirmed Leah's worst fear: She would never be like Rachel. She would never be enough. From Buechner once more, in the words of Jacob:

"And when dawn came ruddy through the walls of the tent, we awoke in each other's arms and my eyes beheld at last the woman I had drowned with… I buried my face in the hot pit of her throat and wept." [27]

Every bride wants to wake up on the morning after her wedding night and bask in the approving, loving eyes of her husband. One look at Leah, and Jacob bolted. He immediately rushed from the wedding tent to confront his deceitful uncle. When he saw how he had been deceived, did Jacob think back to the time he put on a disguise and pretended to be someone else? Did he recall the time he put on Esau's clothes and lied to his blind father? Jacob had truly met his match in Laban.

How Leah must have choked back tears, fear, anger, and self hatred. She saw how furious Jacob was and that he didn't want her. He was very vocal about it with Laban. His displeasure in the morning light set in motion the pattern Leah's life would follow until the day she died. Her worst fears were cemented in her heart: She was not enough.

Read Genesis 29:25-30.

What did Jacob say to Laban?

_____

_____

_____

How did Jacob and Laban amend their previous agreement?

_____

_____

Imagine you are Leah, waiting nervously in the tent for Jacob to return. You start to go outside and look for him, but then you hear screaming from your sister's tent. As you pull back the flap in the tent you see Rachel storming your way. Tears streaming, her face blazing with anger and disbelief, you hear her shouting your name for all to hear.

"Leah!! How could you? Leah!! What have you done?!!"

Who knows what sibling rivalry may have existed before. From this day forward, they would be two sisters struggling down a path in a tug of war that would last for decades.

After reading **verses 27-28**, write in Leah's journal:

_____

_____

_____

Jacob has agreed to "complete the honeymoon week" (The Message). Sounds like every girl's dream honeymoon. Forced intimacy with a man who is in love with the girl one tent down. He would do his duty and keep Leah as his wife. But his heart belonged to Rachel.

Verse 30 is the ultimate knife in Leah's heart. This one verse drives a wedge between them all: Laban and his daughters, Jacob and Leah, Leah and Rachel, all are punished.

Fill in the blanks: "And he _____ Rachel more than _____."

He loved Rachel more than Leah.

Where does Jacob live?

_____

Has Jacob divorced Leah?

_____

Write a few sentences in Leah's journal describing the tension:

_____

_____

_____

We wonder if she might have written something like this:

"Never in my wildest nightmares could I have dreamed my life to be so cursed. Here I am in love with Jacob, and nothing I do will ever please him. His eyes look for Rachel, and he stays with her as much as possible. I hear their laughter in the night air and stifle my own sobs into the pillow. Yesterday, father asked if I was all right. What could he possibly mean? Father is the one who orchestrated this horror and now asks if I am all right? I will never again be all right as long as I live! And Jehovah God, have you completely forgotten me? Am I to live my life as the butt of this sick joke?"

Leah's faith in a loving, sovereign God was put through a blazing fire of doubts. Lonely, without children, aware of Laban's heartless abuse of his daughters to control Jacob, in love with Jacob yet unable to win his affection, painfully estranged from her only sister, Leah would obviously have wondered if God himself even knew she existed.

"Sometimes I ask God, my rock-solid God,
'Why did you let me down?
Why am I walking around in tears,
harassed by enemies?" (Ps. 42:9 The Message)

Times when God seems utterly absent from our circumstances are the hardest to survive. Leah was surrounded by a powerful family, a bevy of servants, wed to a powerful man, yet she is alone. Well, not quite. Let's read of how God assured Leah that he was her very present help in time of trouble.

Go to Genesis 29:31.

How is Leah described?

_____

How does the Lord reveal his presence?

_____

Either Jacob has not come to Leah during her fertile days, used some form of contraception, or she simply has been unable to conceive. Yet the Lord opens her womb to give her children. There's speculation that Jacob, ever the controlling deceiver himself, may have resisted fathering a child with Leah. In doing so he would keep Laban from the satisfaction of having grandchildren in the line of Abraham. He also may not have wanted to burden Rachel with the pain of watching Leah carry his child.

Yet God sees the heart. God knows our pain and every detail of our circumstances. Behind the closed tent, in the wee hours of the morning and night, God saw his daughter Leah despised and afflicted. (One commentary notes that in verse 33, when Leah is described as "unloved," this actually means she was "hated.") [28]

Michael Card once said something to the effect of, "When you see a barren woman in the Bible, look out: God is about to do something huge."

In the barren lives of biblical women, many times God moved mightily to birth children. In the barren heartache of Leah's life, God opened her body to conceive. Whether or not Jacob wanted children with Leah, we cannot know. But in a culture that honored women who were fertile, Leah began popping out sons like Mother Earth. Wives who bore sons for their husbands were considered to be most highly favored.

What was the name of Leah's first son? **Find it in verse 32.**

_____

Leah declared, "The Lord has seen my affliction," and his name means, "See, a son!"

In **verse 33**, she bears her second son:

_____

She declared, "The Lord has heard I am unloved," and his name means, "God hears."

In **verse 34**, what son is born?

_____

His name means "companion."

In **verse 35,** what newborn arrives next?

_____

His name means "praise."

Are you tired? Then rest for a moment. By the end of Genesis 29 we read that Leah ceased bearing, at least for a time. Exhale.

Leah's story could easily be made into a three-hour movie, complete with intermission. We've only just scratched the surface of the main feature coming her way and we admit to being worn out from trying to walk a day in her sandals.

What do you think Leah would want to say to us today? What themes do we hear playing in her life? What lessons learned? What brave places healed in her torn heart?

Leah proclaimed her faith in God in the midst of her pain. Leah may not have felt special or valued but she knew where to go with her problems and she knew who had the power to do something about them. This woman's prayer life must have been serious. She made a habit out of crying out to Jehovah. She knew where to take her heartache. Her sons were named in honor of her one true love.

Jehovah sees and Jehovah hears. There was no way out for Leah but up. And that's exactly where she went. Straight to the top. To the one who had the power to restore her dignity and worth.

Leah never got what she needed from her earthly father. As a little girl, surely she wanted what every little girl wants. She looked for approval and delight in Laban's eyes when he saw her. That look never came. Laban's own words reveal how much he invested in the self-worth of his daughters. In an attempt to calm Jacob after the shock of his wedding night, **read Genesis 29:27.**

How does Laban refer to his daughters?

The NASB translation is the closest to the Old Testament Hebrew. It shows that Laban doesn't even use their names in his conversation with Jacob. To him, they are "this one" and "the other also." Truly he viewed his daughters as property to be bargained and sold.

Yet their heavenly father made sure their names were recorded. It is comforting that the Holy Spirit guided Moses in the writing of this history, for by including the details and stories of so many women, they are elevated to a place of value and high esteem.

Leah has one more courageous insight to give us. It's one of the most powerful lessons any woman can take to heart. Let's read one key mistake our sweet Leah made when she became a mother. **In Genesis 29:32** and **Genesis 30:31-32,** what did Leah assume would happen because of bearing Jacob sons?

It's as though each time she gives birth, she is saying to Jacob, "See me? Do you see me now? Am I good enough? Am I pretty now? Do you love me just a little?" She had no sense of her worth apart from his approval.

Too many women marry thinking they will change their husbands.

Too many buy into the lie that sex or children will give them power over a man's heart. If anything, Leah's story teaches us that, even if we have what our culture sees as "everything," without God we come up short. In her time, to be married with four sons would have been comparable to having it all. Yet Leah could not win the heart of Jacob with a football team of sons.

"Power can do everything but the most important thing: It cannot control love." [29]

In what places are we daily encouraged by our culture to put our trust?

We'll explore this question in detail with Leah's sister, Rachel.

If we place our sole confidence in anything but God, we will be disappointed. We may not end up marrying our sister's fiancé or being hustled by our father, but someone, somewhere, will disappoint us. Someone we love will let us down. Someone closest to us will say or do something that hurts and hangs in the air, or wakes us in the night. We may even be disappointed by God, but he is the only one who sees the heart. He understands our pain. He came to earth to show us how far he would go to give us everything.

Turn to Matthew 11:28.

What does Jesus ask of us?

_____

Come… all who are tired of trying to be something we cannot be, attempting to please others by carrying a heavy burden we were not made to carry. Come…all who need rest, safety, and love. Learn of him. Let go of lost dreams and expectations. Discover abiding love by drinking living water from the well of Christ. Allow the gentle, humble touch of Jesus to lift the weight from our shoulders.

Leah asks us give our hearts to the only one who will treat us forever as his treasured love. In loving Jesus first, we can then open our hearts to a world where inevitable heartbreak will come. Trusting ultimately in God's work, we can risk being tossed and turned, knowing where to take our deepest disappointments. The only sure source of self-worth is found in the eyes of Jesus who alone can heal, restore, and redeem the broken places.

As said by Frances de Sales:"Now the greater our knowledge of our own misery, the more profound will be our confidence in the goodness and mercy of God, for mercy and misery are so closely connected that the one cannot be exercised without the other."

TODAY'S DATE: _____

NOW WRITE YOURSELF A HEADLINE. Listen carefully to the Holy Spirit. How are you inspired by God's lovely Leah?

_____

"On Christ the solid rock I stand
All other ground is sinking sand
All other ground is sinking sand." [30]

"The Solid Rock"

BREAKING NEWS

TV Tattler

THE REAL HOUSEWIVES OF JACOB

This week's episode:
Jacob Changes His Name to Israel

Release of Unseen Film Footage This Friday Night at 8 p. m. Middle Eastern Time

The Real Housewives of Jacob has been a runaway hit series for the past ten seasons. People just can't get enough of the ongoing saga that started with the splashy reality show, *Life with the Laban Clan: Can't They All Just Get Along?* For years we've watched this family clamor and claw their way through legal claims swirling around who is the rightful wife of Jacob.

After the matter was settled out of court, the drama has only deepened. For ten years now, Jacob has beaten the odds. The majority of the marriage counseling community never believed he would be able to sustain a marriage between two wives, both sisters who are so radically different in personality and style. Much like watching a car wreck, we can't seem to tear ourselves away from the ever-changing details of Jacob's dynamic, dysfunctional family.

And now reports surface that Jacob is changing his name. He insists on being called "Israel." Has he cracked under pressure? Is he changing his name as a first move in divorce proceedings from one of the wives? Child support alone for Leah's brood would cost him a fortune.

At present count, Leah, the eldest sister and victim of the infamous wife swap, has given birth to a posse of children. She seems to be on a mission to secure her position in Jacob's will and to keep a strong upper hand as head mistress of the house. Rachel, claiming to be the only woman Jacob has ever loved, remains childless. She recently was pictured on the cover of *People of the East's Top 50 Most Beautiful People* issue. This would be Rachel's fifth cover issue and, unlike her elder sister, Rachel is not put off by media attention.

Questions surfaced this week when Rachel was spotted leaving the office of one of the country's top infertility clinics. One of the doctor's assistants (who asked to remain anonymous) reported that Rachel was interested in the use of mandrakes, more commonly known as love apples, for conception. The effectiveness of love apples as a fertility aid is unsubstantiated and mostly dismissed as a superstitious old wives' tale. *"Rachel looked stunning, just like you've seen her on* TV," said the nurse, "But she was extremely agitated when the doctor told her there was nothing he could do. She was crying when she slipped out the back door."

Now, on the heels of this report, we have learned that this Friday night, never-before-seen film footage of the family will be aired on primetime television. There are rumors that for the first time the syndicated program will release interviews from Zilpah and Bilhah, Jacob's concubines and attendants to Leah and Rachel. Obviously, hearing from the two concubines will drive the show's ratings to an all-time high.

Jacob may or may not take advantage of the primetime coverage to explain the mysterious change of his name. We all have heard rumors of his strange dreams and fixation on angels. Years earlier Jacob claimed he had visions of angels moving up and down a ladder to heaven. Now come explosive reports that Jacob claims to have personally wrestled with an angel all night. Many believe he has become delusional, while others close to the family say he is a changed man.

On a completely different note, Leah and Rachel were seen having lunch last week without the usual hubbub of children and handlers. The restaurant owner said they sat in a private booth and seemed to be having a delightful time, laughing and talking for hours. *"The staff worked very hard to give them their privacy,"* said Chef Obal. *"But I was moved at one point when I looked over to see them holding hands, heads bowed...* as if they were... praying?"

Tune in this Friday night to view more details about this increasingly intriguing family.

I will pour out My Spirit into your children, and My blessing on your descendants. Your children will grow like a tree in the grass, like poplar trees growing beside streams of water. Isa. 44:3-4 New Century Version

TODAY'S HEROINE:

Rachel, mother of Joseph and Benjamin, wife of Jacob, daughter of Laban, sister of Leah

We have purposefully allowed our imaginations to wander back into another culture. Aware that we have little embellishment from Scripture, we can still respectfully ask God to help us imagine life in Laban's family. As women who seek God through his Word, we ask him to reveal truth for us today as we mentally enter the house of Jacob, the tents of Rachel and Leah, and relate to them as flesh-and-blood people.

Today's brave sister has our heads spinning. With the help of coffee, magazines, commentaries, and more translations of the Bible than usual, our fingers simply won't type fast enough. Maybe it's the coffee, or a rush of adrenaline from reading **Genesis 29-34!**

Bonnie's husband Brent had an insightful observation we'd like to share with you. "Before Brent left the house this morning I had to talk about Rachel," Bonnie said. "Words spilled out about the tension between Rachel and Leah, and the battle over Jacob, and the deception of Laban, and the pain in their lives. Brent listened patiently and then said, 'You know I hear people today saying we have trouble in our lives and situations that no one has ever experienced before and it's a different day and time now. We should all read through some of Genesis and remember there is nothing new under the sun!'"

Amen. The drama of Rachel and Leah's love for Jacob can make your blood pressure rise by the minute. They lived lives as riveting as any Tennessee Williams drama, breathtaking as any romance novel, and as complicated as the most outrageous soap opera. How on earth did they survive? How do any of us who trust God survive? We hang on for dear life. We hold on until at last we realize that it is he who holds us.

Rachel held on like a tiger. Much like Leah, their tug of war was an equal match of wills. These two sisters were forced into a duel of the heart, both searching for a way to please the love of their lives. Both were infected by the human disease of believing 'I will never be enough.' The virus of female insecurity has no vaccine. We all are susceptible to infection. The only cure is found in receiving God's never-ending affirmation.

As we study together, please keep this in the forefront of your mind: **These two daughters are birthing God's dream!** No matter how disjointed or insane the process, whether or not they are aware of the outcome, Rachel and Leah are on God's path. They are part of a huge picture. **These two warring sisters, married to a dreamer, are God's dream girls.**

What were Rachel's dreams? As a Middle Eastern woman of this time, her hopes were set on marrying and bearing children. Like Leah, her identity was completely bound up in her ability to have children. When she was growing up, did she lie in her tent at night and fantasize about the kind of man her father would arrange for her to marry? Like Leah, did she wonder what it would be like to have children? Like you and me, did she hope for daughters to laugh with and help with the work, and for sons who would carry on the family name? Common ground we women walk, this sharing of hope-filled dreams. We long for love, for acceptance, for children, and too often, we look to a man alone to complete our dreams.

Jacob was caught in a no-win situation. He never would be enough, nor would the women in his life ever feel they were enough for him. In the stories of his two wives, we find the hard-learned lesson that only in God can we be fulfilled. Some truths come to us easily. Others come after a serious dose of heartache.

Our hearts ache, too, as we move into the years-long struggle between Leah and Rachel. Perhaps it began when they were children. As noted in our previous lesson, there is no mention of Laban's wife. Nowhere is a wife mentioned, either in the negotiations of the marriage, at the wedding ceremony, or during the birth of the grandchildren. We can safely assume Leah would have been "responsible" for Rachel. She was the older babysitter, watching out for her younger sister.

My (Bonnie's) children are four and a half years apart, Courtney older than her younger brother, Graham. I have so many momma memories of them growing up and, like most kids, duking it out from time to time. One of our favorite family memories is of the times Courtney would trip Graham as he walked by. Every once in a while, one of her long legs would quickly dart out at just the right moment and Graham would take a spill. Courtney would laugh with devious delight. And Graham, being such a guileless child, was oblivious to anything but his love for his sister. He would simply laugh right along with his big sister. He adored Courtney, following her around and wanting to do everything she was doing. Sometimes this made her crazy. Most of the time, she took full advantage of his undivided attention. As they've grown into adulthood, I am grateful for their close hearts and tight friendship.

I am the oldest of three children. We had our moments of rough-and-tumble, but the three of us share an abiding love for each other. My brother Stan is three years younger, so I had lots of fun bossing him around until he grew up—and up—and towered over me. Then I began to back off and "enjoy" his company in a more balanced way. However, my younger sister, Amy, was like a toy to me. She is seven years younger. I dressed her up like a doll, called her "Princess," and helped spoil her rotten.

Makes us wonder if Leah and Rachel had a fairly good start of things. Did they play together in their youth? Perhaps Leah dressed up her younger sister and called her "Princess," too. Then as time went on, and Laban treated his daughters as property rather than treasures, did Leah resent having to make sure Rachel's scraped knees were cleaned and her hair brushed? By the time they were of marriage age, did a full out rivalry ensue? It seems inevitable that their differences would one day threaten their relationship.

Rachel was the golden child. She was beautiful, favored, and younger. Leah's name, remember, meant "wild cow," and she was described as weak-eyed and dull.

For a quick reminder, **read Genesis 29:17.**

How is Rachel described?

Her name was a term of endearment meaning "ewe lamb." [31] She would have been the popular girl in school, the homecoming queen, head of the cheerleading squad. People meeting Leah and Rachel for the first time might have commented, "You two are sisters? Really? You don't look a thing alike!"

Rachel easily might have been one of those smiling faces whispering from advertisements, "Don't hate me because I'm beautiful." Do you wonder if from time to time, Leah wanted to slap her silly?

Who knows what happened to cause the bride swap in Genesis 29:22-23? Let's try for the sake of good girl-talk to think this through.

Refresh your memory by reading Genesis 29:1-11.

Jacob arrived in the land of Nahor with a stolen blessing from his father Isaac. Jacob cleverly concealed his identity. An aging, blind Isaac unknowingly passed the Abrahamic blessing onto Jacob and sent him off to the land of Haran to live out God's will for his life.

Jacob arrived in Uncle Laban's stomping ground and quickly met the love of his life. Rarely in the Bible is such a public display of affection recorded. Jacob physically sweeps Rachel off her feet. He certainly adored her.

What was Rachel's vocation? **Find it in verse 9.**

_____

How would you describe Jacob's response when he realized who Rachel was?

_____

_____

_____

According to **verse 11**, what did Jacob do after watering the sheep?

_____

_____

Like a dashing Prince Charming from the best Disney movie, Jacob claims his bride. Rachel was surely impressed. A complete stranger moves back the heavy stone from the well, revealing a few muscles in the process, then offers to water the flock for her. After completing this act of chivalry, he kisses her and begins to cry. If Rachel wanted a man unafraid to show his feelings, Jacob was her dream come true.

From last week's lesson we know that Jacob declared his love for Rachel and agreed to work for seven years for her hand in marriage. He took up residence on Laban's estate, and for Jacob, the years passed quickly. Rachel must have felt cherished and special for a man to devote himself to hard labor in order to be her husband. Her healthy self image was now strengthened by the long public display of commitment by Jacob.

Suspend your disbelief because we live in a culture that would laugh this engagement off the calendar. Let's just go with the scenario. For seven years imagine the longing glances between Rachel and Jacob, the stolen moments holding hands after dark behind the tent, the anticipation of building their lives together, this long Bolero dance of romance.

All the while, Leah stands by watching her younger sister's love story unfolding. Remember there is nothing written about a marriage for Leah. Was Rachel aware what this engagement period cost her older sister?

To be fair to Leah, let's write a little in "Rachel's journal:"

_____

_____

_____

_____

Here's our version: *"Dear Diary, I can't believe it's true! Jacob is so handsome and charming*, and the way he looks at me melts me into a puddle. Everyone is talking about the wedding and my bridal gown is stunning! How could I be so blessed to be marrying the son of Uncle Isaac? Everything feels perfect, simply perfect. I have never been so happy! The whole world seems to be spinning around me! It's all about me!"

Well, maybe Rachel wasn't quite so vapid. But she was accustomed to her role of being the prettiest, favored daughter and was now publicly engaged to a wealthy, God-favored cousin. At the end of the seven years, we almost can feel the tension rise to a fevered pitch.

Jacob has fulfilled his obligations. It's party time. Let the wedding ceremonies begin. And so they do. Laban throws a party, and the men gather. We don't know what happened, but commentaries suggest there would have been days of celebration, and nights of flowing wine.

No season of *Bridezillas* compares to the nightmare that followed. Jacob waited for his bride. Laban delivered. Only he delivered the elder sister, Leah.

EDITORIAL: A fascinating piece of information on the history of the veil. According to Jewish wedding history, the custom of veiling a bride (badecken) dates back to Rebekah (Rebecca) in Genesis 24:65: "Rebecca took her veil and concealed herself with it" upon meeting her fiance, Isaac. Then along comes the fiasco on Jacob's wedding night. Afterward to avoid such a mishap, according to Jewish legend, the groom 'checks' to be sure that it is indeed his bride, before her veil is lowered over her face. [32]

As women, can we all agree that, of all the questions we have about the infamous bride swap, the most burning question has to be: Where in the world was Rachel during the wedding celebration?

Did Laban send her away on an "errand?" Was she tied up and gagged in her tent until after the wedding night? Did she go to visit a friend or relative and miss the wedding all together? If she was home, then how is it that she was not being adorned in her bridal gown, in the bridal tent by the attendants? Did she agree to the deceit as well? Were Rachel and Leah forced to do their father's will, even at the price of betraying themselves? Why didn't Rachel warn Jacob? From their mansions in heaven one can imagine a long line of women eager to hear the rest of the story!

We do know that Jacob went ballistic when we woke up after his honeymoon night to find Leah in his bed. He agreed to work seven more years (cunning Laban) for the right to marry Rachel.

In **verse 30,** what grand canyon now divided Rachel and Leah?

_____

_____

Jacob himself. Jacob loved Rachel. Jacob tolerated Leah. Jacob became the great divide.

"Never, never pin your whole faith on any human being: not if he is the best and wisest in the whole world," wrote C. S. Lewis. "There are lots of nice things you can do with sand; but do not try building a house on it."[33] As we leave Genesis 29, we find the sisters move full throttle into high gear in a battle to win Jacob's love. The first one to have his child would surely be the most favored wife. Leah won this contest hands down. God saw her state of despair and opened her womb. She had four sons back to back and named each one as victory cry: "See, a son!" "God hears," "companion," and "praise." Leah assumed she had found the key to wooing Jacob away from her sister Rachel.

The last half of **Genesis 29:31** gives us insight into Rachel's agony.

What does this say about the physically beautiful bride?

_____

_____

Suddenly we find Rachel and Leah on equal emotional footing. Both women are barren; one in body, the other in soul. Both believe children are the key to securing Jacob's love. Yet Leah, who easily bore Jacob sons, could not win his heart. And Rachel, who made his heart pound with desire, could give him no children of their own.

Neither woman feels she is enough.

The need for male approval is pain they share. Neither of these sisters ever pleased their father, or received his praises. Laban saw his daughters as property. One step up from cattle, they could fetch a handsome bargain if he played his cards right. Leah and Rachel were pawns in Laban's chess game. Two precious women used for collateral.

There are other examples in Scripture of fathers offering their daughters in exchange for something they need.

Read Joshua 15:16-17.

What was Caleb's offer to the bachelors in his army?

___

Read 1 Samuel 17:20-25.

What did Saul offer to the man who could kill Goliath?

___

Read Genesis 19:4-8.

What did Lot offer the men of Sodom and Gomorrah?

___

___

If you didn't get the nurturing you needed from your father, you're not alone. Since the Garden of Eden and our fall into sin, fathers have been neglecting and hurting their daughters. Those scars are often carried into adulthood, where the little girl still needing male security looks for worth and validation in all the wrong places.

Here we find our brave sisters doing the best they can while still aching for male affirmation. Leah had a house full of crying children, but wept into the night without Jacob in her bed. And consider Rachel the next time you see a beautiful woman and assume she has everything coming up roses. Her physical beauty won the love of Jacob, but she remained childless.

Rachel may have been the most worked-for bride in history, but she could not give her husband a child. We all have a hole in our souls that only God can fill. And we each have a time in which we find our most charming selves, our winning smile, our most well-written term paper, or our attempts to achieve fall flat in the end.

Leah may have had weak eyes, but she was one fertile lady. Rachel, for all her beauty and favor, was barren. Now who was the favored daughter? Wives who gave their husbands sons were considered blessed. The scales of justice begin to tip in Leah's direction and away from the flawless face of her sister. Leah has finally found something that Rachel could not give Jacob: sons.

Let's do a review of Leah's assumptions.

Genesis 29:32: "Surely my husband will love me now" (NIV). **Genesis 29:34**: Now at last my husband will become attached to me, because I have borne him three sons" (NIV). Leah has a head start in the baby race, while Rachel has yet to have her first wave of morning sickness.

Take a deep breath, get out a pencil and keep score as you read **Genesis 30:1-24.**

The Grand Baby Race between Leah and Rachel: And...they're off!

By the time Rachel gives birth to Joseph in **verse 24**, we are completely worn out. Their man Jacob was one busy dude. From tent to tent, wife to wife, concubine to concubine, the baby race was on.

For those of you who have suffered through an agonizing season of infertility, your heart must be resonating with our dear Rachel. It's excruciating to be a woman who wants to be a mother and is unable to have a child. The whole world looks like a sea of children and you wonder why you haven't gotten pregnant. Is it something in your diet? In your past? Some grievance God has against you? Some cross you are supposed to bear? Worse still, maybe God knows you wouldn't be a good mother.

In **Genesis 30: 1-2**, how did Rachel respond to her problem?

_____

_____

She argued with Jacob. She was jealous of Leah. She demanded that Jacob solve the problem or else she would jump off the nearest cliff. In **Genesis 30: 2**, Jacob's anger is described as his nose turning red.

Levitical laws were not yet in place, but if there were rites of purification, Rachel had it even tougher. In ancient times she might have been forbidden to have intimacy with her husband during her menstrual cycle. Then after the cycle, there could have been days of purification where she would still be off-limits for her husband. If you do the math, there were perhaps two weeks during which she could have been with Jacob, and out of those two weeks, only twenty-four to forty-eight hours when she was ovulating.

For those of us who live with sisters, or work around girlfriends on a consistent basis, we know that many times, our cycles will sync up. We'll have our cycle during the same week. Did Rachel also have this unwanted gift of timing with her sister Leah? It would have made the miracle of Leah's children all the harder to bear, and intensified the competition of sharing of Jacob during Rachel's fertile days.

From Buechner's book, *The Son of Laughter*, in the voice of Jacob, Buechner describes what very well may have happened. (In his writing, based on Genesis 31: 42, Jacob refers to God as "the Fear.")

*"My seed was in her (Rachel) belly, but her belly proved to be barren. The bitterness of Leah at having no children became now Rachel's bitterness and mine. It was the Fear's revenge. Months went by without Rachel's conceiving. By rights I should have spent one night with her and the next night with her sister, but inste*ad I spent six nights out of every seven with Rachel and only the one with Leah. It was not only that Rachel was the one I loved, but I did not want to waste my seed on anyone else. Leah was enraged. She spat on the ground whenever Rachel showed her face....

We were all at odds with each other. Rachel grew thinner and thinner thinking that she was barren and that her sister hated her. Leah in her humiliation grew fatter, stuffing herself with food to make up for all the ways she charged me with starving her.... Laban was angry at all three of us for giving him no grandchildren...."[34]

Can you relate to Rachel's frustration with unanswered prayer?

_____

_____

Read Proverbs 19:21.

Apply this verse to Rachel.

_____

_____

_____

I (Nan) can testify from personal experience what it's like to ride the infertility roller coaster. I don't remember ever telling my husband I would die if he didn't give me children, but I do remember the helpless feelings and frustration when month after month we couldn't conceive.

After years of living by my monthly cycle and taking my temperature on a daily basis in an attempt to "time" everything perfectly, as well as numerous doctor visits and medications, I came to the conclusion that, apart from a miracle, I was never going to experience childbirth.

I remember one day in particular, standing at my kitchen sink, looking out the window. Wayne and I had been through every known infertility procedure that our budget would allow and still we had no baby. I knew it wouldn't be difficult for God to give us children. After all, the Scriptures are full of stories of infertile women getting pregnant without the aid of drugs or surgery. So I prayed, "Father, it would be easy for you to work a miracle and allow us to conceive. You specialize in making barren women pregnant even when they're ninety years old! So if you're not going to give us children right now, then please take away my desire for them, because I don't want to be discontent with whatever plans you have for me. I want to be content with my circumstances."

Before I'd even finished the prayer, he answered. I felt a burden lift. I was free. I knew God was aware of my situation and was being very intentional with me, so I began to rest in my circumstances. Our friends were all having children and were sensitive to our situation. I was often the last person to be told when someone discovered they were pregnant. And many were afraid to invite me to baby showers. I knew they were trying to keep me from being hurt, but I was truly happy for their good news and wanted to share their joy. God had given me so much peace that I was not jealous of their good fortune. (I also have some adorable nieces and nephews that helped give me a place for my maternal instincts.)

Aside from the occasional irritating experience of nosy people asking us why we didn't have children, we handled our infertility pretty well. But I did have one experience that helped me see how Rachel must have felt.

I traveled to a Central American country on a mission trip one summer and taught Vacation Bible School in a small church. The local people were friendly and curious about our personal lives. One day, a man in the church asked me, in front of other people, if I had children. I smiled and said, "No." Then he looked at me and with a pronouncement of a curse replied, "A dry branch will be cut off."

My first reaction was to counter with a verbal equivalent of a right hook to his jaw. Thankfully, I didn't say anything I would regret. I didn't owe him any details as to why I was childless, so I just walked away. However, I was struck not only by his rudeness, but also by his lack of perception of the value of a woman.

I always have known that my worth is not bound up in my ability to conceive. I am a twenty-first century woman with all kinds of opportunities for work and fulfillment. My self-worth is not limited to my fertility. But that was not true for Rachel. She saw herself in the same way that the Central American man saw me: dry and useless. In Rachel's case, the stakes were very high. In her time, a woman could be divorced if she failed to conceive.

Rachel didn't have the words of **Psalms 139:13-16** to comfort her.

In Psalm 139:13, how does David describe the process God used to create him in his mother's womb?

_____

_____

_____

Rachel strongly would have identified with the process of weaving. It is all together slow, painstaking, and deliberate. Nothing is left to chance. Nothing is accidental. The choices of thread are made one at a time. The phrase, "I am fearfully and wonderfully made" can be rephrased as, "I am an awesome wonder." [35]

How might this truth have given Rachel peace?

_____

_____

Do you think it was conceited for David to think of himself as an awesome wonder?

_____

Is it difficult to see yourself this way?

_____

God put you together one cell at a time, and he is very pleased with you. He doesn't require you to perform or achieve anything before he delights in you. He delighted in your tiniest form as it developed in your mother's womb. If this is what the God of the universe thinks of us, it is wise for us to agree with him.

My story (Nan's) took a turn that I never expected, but like Rachel, I had to wait for God's timing. Twenty-one years after I stood at my kitchen window and asked for help, I was doing the Henry Blackaby Bible study, *Experiencing God*. (Let me say if you have not done this study, I highly recommend it.) Blackaby teaches that God is at work all the time in the lives of the people around us. My homework on May 15, 1996, was to ask God to show me where he was at work in the life of someone near me, and when he did, that would be my invitation to come alongside him in that work.

I thought that sounded pretty easy, so I asked God to show me where he was at work in my husband's life, and if he would show me, I would do my best to help. Then I went about my day and forgot about my prayer. That evening, after dinner, I went outside and began planting some flowers around the border of our patio. Wayne came out and sat down. After a moment, he began weeping. (Now let me make something very clear: Wayne **never** comes out onto the patio and weeps.) Then he said, "Nan, are you aware of what is happening to the baby girls in China? I think we ought to talk about adopting."

To say I was astonished is the understatement of the year. At that moment, it was safe to assume that God was definitely **at work**! I quickly got up out of the dirt in our flower border and sat down beside him. We talked for a long time and decided right then to begin the process of adoption. Then I remembered the prayer I'd prayed that morning, and I knew beyond any doubt this was God's will, and that he already had picked out a baby for us who was halfway around the world.

The maternal instincts that I had asked God to remove from me twenty-one years prior came roaring back with a vengeance! I couldn't wait to be a mom! I began the nesting process of preparing a nursery, and all those dear friends who had wished for me to be a mother now lined up to give us baby showers. It was a time of great joy and a time of much paperwork and more waiting. But God fulfilled his word to me and now we are the grateful parents of two beautiful daughters from China.

Our infertility was used by God to bring us to maturity and to give a home to two adorable girls who otherwise would have had a life without loving parents. Looking back on my journey through infertility, I wouldn't change a thing.

An infertile modern woman has options. Rachel had none. So she began to bargain. Enter the concubine and the mandrakes, and the race heats up.

In Genesis 30:3, what deal does Rachel make with Jacob?

_____

_____

The phrase "bear upon my knees" refers to the process of legally adopting the children borne by your concubines. They officially become the children of the wife. Rachel knows her shame of being childless will be removed if her handmaid bears a child by Jacob.

What was this like for Jacob? He was sleeping with four different women. Sounds like some men's idea of a great set up. But each woman looked to him to give them a child for identity, for significance, for confidence, for redemption. He knew the promise God had made to his grandfather Abraham about his descendants multiplying as the stars of the heavens and as the sand on the seashore. Jacob must have wondered if God's promise was going to be fulfilled from his very loins in his lifetime!

The intensity of the competition between the sisters for his "seed" moves speedily from the involvement of concubines and into bargaining over mandrakes.

In verses 14-16, what deal does Rachel make with Leah?

_____

_____

_____

Mandrakes were plants superstitiously thought to enhance fertility. Rachel wanted the mandrakes, hoping they would work magic for her and cause her to conceive. Love apples are now center stage.

How does Leah counter this request in **verse 15**?

_____

_____

We hear shades of Laban in his eldest daughter's words. "You took my husband and now you want my son's mandrakes?" Who took whose husband? (This is where some good old-fashioned hair pulling would be a reasonable response from Rachel.)

Desperate times can bring out the worst in anyone. Rachel was willing to barter a night in her husband's bed in exchange for a magic apple. "You take Jacob for the night," she might have said. I want the mandrakes so I can become pregnant." Leah agreed to give Rachel the apples in exchange for an extra night with their man Jacob. Mandrakes gave Rachel the hope of getting pregnant and gave Leah another chance at getting Jacob's attention. Another deal brokered between the warring sisters.

Leah meets Jacob as he comes in from the field that night and tells him he "must" have sex with her. It seems particularly sad that Leah resorts to "hiring" Jacob to sleep with her. He would fulfill his marital duties to Leah, but she knows his heart is not in it. Leah is still hoping that Jacob will one day love her.

Read Genesis 30:20.

"This time my husband will treat me with honor, because I have borne him six sons" (NIV). The Amplified Bible spells it out as "regard me as his wife in reality."

Whose birth is recorded in **verse 21**?

_____

What proclamation or words of praise and victory come from Leah as her only daughter is born?

_____

Unfortunately, you were not able to write anything in the preceding blank. Leah has been the vessel through which God gave Jacob ten sons, and at last a daughter is born. Yet no one has anything to say about Dinah. The birth of a daughter was not cause for celebration.

How well Leah and Rachel knew this to be true. Leah could not affirm her daughter in ways that she herself had not been affirmed. And so the cycle of not being enough is passed from mother to daughter and goes on and on for women from one generation to the next.

It will continue unless we turn our eyes upon Jesus and look full in his wonderful face. He died on that tree so that we can fall farther from our own family tree. In Christ, each of us has the chance to learn from generations past, and to change the way we respond to our husbands, to our children, to our lives this side of heaven.

We have immersed ourselves for the past two chapters in one very messed-up family. **God's mercy for them in the midst of their fallen state is our treasure.** Rachel and Leah, Jacob and his heirs, have much to teach us about the complete and mysterious lunacy of God's love. Rich Mullins' song lyric about the "reckless, raging fury they call the love of God" comes to mind. For God so loved this scheming, lying, desperate, insecure, jockeying family, that through them, he birthed the Hebrew nation!

Now, take a moment and read this next sentence. Read it aloud.

I have studied the birth of the twelve tribes of Israel.

Astonishing, is it not? From Leah and Rachel warring over Jacob, bartering over love apples and tossing concubines into his tent, twelve sons of Israel are born. If God can work with that, sweet one, then he can most definitely work with anything you and I face today.

Rachel, our beauty queen, teaches us that no matter how dark the pit, God honored his promise to bring forth people to call his own. The fallen state of man never has handicapped God. In spite of us, God works. He always and continually is at work.

Turn for a moment to read **Philippians 2:13**. What does this verse speak to you, right where you live today?

_____

_____

"(Not in your own strength) for it is God Who all the while is effectually at work in you (energizing and creating in you the power and desire), both to will and to work for His good pleasure and satisfaction and delight" (Amplified Bible).

Not by might, not by power, but by my Spirit, says the Lord.

Rachel could not win and keep the love of Jacob, no matter how much she batted her lovely eyes and mastered the art of seduction. Leah could not win the love of Jacob no matter how many babies she paraded before him in their strollers. Only God could use these women to complete his good and perfect work. Only God could effectually use their feeble attempts to find love and to find him.

What do our sisters in Genesis have to say to us today? Why does their story matter? Rachel and Leah embody every insecurity a woman can face. We are so quick to think, "I'm not pretty enough. I'm not smart enough. I'm not talented enough. Not old enough… or young enough…."We believe these sisters are saying,"Enough is enough!"

None of us feels like we are enough. So there; let's admit it and move on. We all set standards for ourselves, spoken and unspoken. How often do we compare ourselves to the faces on the covers of magazines? How many times do we stand in line at the grocery store, glance at the magazine rack, and leave feeling depressed and hopeless about our weight, hairstyle, teeth, or wardrobe? The list goes on. We go through life buying into a lie that we are not enough, that we don't measure up, that we'll never be good enough.

Is this what Jesus died for? Setting us free from sin also should include freedom from the tyranny of feeling worthless and the demon of comparison. During Jesus' lifetime on earth, he made a point of treating women with dignity and respect. He interacted with them, addressed them as equals, and welcomed them into his closest circle. The fact that Mary of Bethany was free to sit at his feet and listen to his teaching was revolutionary for that time.

Our savior never intended for us to keep our focus on ourselves and be constantly discontent. If we're forever checking ourselves in the mirror and unhappy with what we see, we'll never get past the endless cycle of diets and face-lifts.

The Scriptures say we are enough in Jesus. God says we are enough. It's time we embrace our "enough stuff!"

Like Rachel, we can learn from our mistaken assumptions. Over time, pain taught her to love God more than anything or anyone else in her life. By the time Joseph was born, we find mature wisdom in Rachel's response.

At last, without seeking man's approval, without wishing and hoping and planning and scheming, **read Genesis 30:24** and note the response from Rachel about the birth of her firstborn son:

_____

_____

Notice that Rachel doesn't mention Jacob, only God. She praises God for taking away her reproach, disgrace, and humiliation. With a heart of faith, she believes and boldly asks that God grant her another son. (In **Genesis 35:16-19,** the Bible records the answer to this prayer, the birth of Benjamin.)

After the birth of Joseph, Jacob finds the courage to break away from Laban. He asks Laban for permission to return to his father's country, insisting that he take his wife and children with him. Jacob is on the brink of a major life change. Not a mid-life crisis, but a mid-life breakthrough. He will at last wrestle with God and be blessed for his tenacity. As with the birth of Tamar's son, any breaking forth is a difficult process.

Laban tries more negotiations, and Jacob has a few missteps. But all in all, God changes and moves his man forward, one step at a time.

The chapters of **Genesis 31-33** record more breathtaking drama in the lives of God's chosen family. We could stop and write a novel right about now, but we have more brave women to discover!

Please note, however, the alliance of our two sisters in **Genesis 31:14**. Jacob has decided to move and is discussing the situation with his family, much like we would in our homes today. How is Jacob answered?

Yes, "Rachel and Leah" answer him. They too stand on the threshold of fresh independence and healing. Their father never had treated them with respect or dignity. Both women now are unified in following Jacob to a new homeland. It hasn't been an easy ride for either sister, and we can't help but smile as they answer with one voice. At last they have bridged the grand canyon that once separated them.

Have they now set their sights on a future beyond Jacob?

Have the births of their children cooled the jealous rivalry and bonded their bloodline with a God-inspired purpose? Have Rachel and Leah realized they are caught up in a bigger picture of God's plan? Their man Jacob did come from the line of Abraham. Perhaps between the bickering and jockeying for Jacob's heart, they heard the heart of God beating stronger, louder, and with more clarity. Like any woman of faith, they discovered the arms of God. His arms will never fail or disappoint. These two sisters were given God's grace to make the whole, disjointed, crazy thing work out.

In studying their lives, we grow to love and admire these two sisters, Leah and Rachel. We identify with their fears and their victories. We agonize with Leah over seasons in our lives when we felt like the biggest *Glamour* "don't" on the planet. For those of us without husbands—whether from divorce, widowhood, or unwanted singleness—we agonize with Rachel when regardless of physical beauty, there was no way to change our circumstances. They have drawn deeply from the well of "not enough" and led every willing woman to the arms of her one true love.

Read Zephaniah 3:14-17.

In this glorious passage, God refers to his people in an affectionate way. He calls them "daughter." He tells them not to give in to a posture of defeat and fear. He calls them to rejoice. Why? Because he is with them and rejoicing in them. He literally sings over them with joy.

God doesn't call them "sons." He calls them "daughter!" This is an amazing validation of our worth as women, as children of God. Because of this truth, what does he invite us to do in **Zephaniah 3:1**?

Yes! So lift up your head and sing, beloved daughter.

You are enough.

If you have a daughter, granddaughter, a mother, a niece, sister, or any young lady who looks up to you, please see it as a gift and privilege to tell them how precious they are in your eyes and in the eyes of the father who dances and sings over them with delight.

We close their story hoping that Leah and Rachel had a growing sense of themselves and their place in history. One day we will ask them if they were able to reconcile and end the years of their lives as true sisters of the heart.

Truly, Laban did not have the last word when it came to the worth of these daughters of the king. From "this one" came the messiah. From the "other one" came Joseph. The value of these women was great in the eyes of God. Maybe we can learn to see ourselves this way too.

Beloved daughter of God, how does this verse specifically encourage you?

_____

_____

_____

Like Rachel and Leah we all are created to hear God singing over us with delight. We are created by a huge God to dream big dreams. Because of the love of Jesus, we are his dream girls.

TODAY'S DATE: _____

YOUR HEADLINE:

_____

Take note of God's lovely Rachel and what she has taught you about how much you are treasured.

> **"I sing for you my beloved**
> Day by day a rhapsody of grace,
> The heavens rejoice at the sound of your name
> I sing for you, over you, my beloved." [36]

"My Beloved" by Bonnie Keen and David Hamilton

THE PLEDGE of "I AM ENOUGH"

Girlfriends, it's time for a little fun. Pour a glass of your favorite beverage and hold it high as you recite the following pledge together. Then toast one another and pray that each of you will live, from this day forward, with the knowledge that you are enough!

I_____(your name) pledge to see myself as God sees me and no longer compare myself to unrealistic and air-brushed women on the covers of magazines.

I will no longer feel guilty about not having sexy, shiny, bouncy, healthy hair.

I will believe that I am wonderfully made even if I don't wear size eight jeans.

I pledge to set my thoughts on things above instead of:

> face-lifts,
> Botox and Restalyne
> Sculptra
> glycolic peels
> liposuction
> collagen injections
> microdermabrasion
> augmentation
> and laser surgery.

From this day forward I will see my wrinkles as evidence of all the laughter in my life.

I will no longer use the term "crow's feet." The crows can keep their feet. I will now refer to them as "lovely arrows pointing to the windows of my soul."

I will celebrate forehead lines, lip lines, smile lines, marionette lines, sagging skin, age spots, and dry skin. In the words of Monty Python, "I'm not dead yet!"

I will not force myself to volumize, minimize, maximize or super-size my lips, hips, hair, or eyelashes.

I will no longer limit my gestures and hide my hands when I need a manicure. In warm weather, this also applies to my feet. Furthermore, I promise to use up all the nail polish I have at home before buying the latest OPI line.

I will pledge to wear shoes that feel good on my feet regardless of how they make my calves or ankles look. Instead of a stiletto strategy, I pledge to support my arches and give my toes the room they deserve.

I refuse to wear clothes that make it a challenge to walk, sit, or bend.

I refuse to weigh myself daily and overanalyze every morsel of food I put into my mouth. I will taste and see that God made chocolate, wine, lobster, home-grown tomatoes, pasta, and artichokes, and with him say, "Yea verily, it is good!"

I will not mentally or physically obsess over lifting, tucking, hoisting, or hiding any of my body parts. I will resist the urge to buy hideously binding, uncomfortable, and expensive underwear that cuts off circulation, constricts vital organs and makes me miserable.

If it's on my body and headed south, I will not force it to make a U-turn.

I will delight in anything on me that wobbles and shakes. It's proof that I'm still here and able to walk, for which I am thankful.

I pledge to wear my age spots as a badge of honor, for they prove I've lived long enough to wise up and not let America's glamour industry ruin my self image.

I pledge to be thankful for what is in my closet instead of constantly discontent with what I wear.

I pledge to stop comparing myself to other women and to be grateful for how God made me.

AS OF THIS MOMENT, I WILL BELIEVE I AM GOD'S WOMAN, I AM FREE,
HEAR ME ROAR! IN JESUS CHRIST, I AM ENOUGH!

(Now lift your glass with one hand, and with your other, grab a love handle and let out your best Middle Eastern high-pitched throat warble!)

BREAKING NEWS

The Persian Pulse

NATIONAL BEAUTY CONTEST TO BE HELD IN PERSIA

King Holding Interviews For New Queen
486-465 B.C.

Reporting from Sushan capital, court of King Xerxes:

Citizens in the Persian capital woke this morning to news of a national search for a new queen of Persia. This follows a humiliating scene at the recent 180 day banquet hosted by King Xerxes. When Queen Vashti refused to parade before the royal officials and military leaders, Xerxes sent his queen into exile and declared he'd find another. The national search for her replacement begins immediately.

King Xerxes has released a formal statement:

"I wear the robe in this household and if Vashti won't obey me, I'll find someone who will. It's for the good of the country. Vashti has wronged not only me but all the men in Persia. If I don't put my foot down, the Queen's behavior will set a bad example for all the women in Per-

sia. Soon every wife will disrespect her husband. It would be chaos!"

Insiders close to Queen Vashti report she defiantly defends her position, "I refuse to be his arm candy! I pity the girl who takes my place. She's welcome to every tiara in my closet!"

King Xerxes finished with another shocking revelation:"Let it also be known that all beautiful young virgins from all 127 provinces are eligible. The one who pleases me most will be my new queen."

Pageant Director Hegai will begin interviews immediately. All contestants will need a current headshot and resume. There will be swimsuit competition. No talent category required. Hegai told the Pulse:"finalists will compete on Bachelorette Season 496 B. C. The whole world will be watching!"

The Persian Pulse will continue to follow this intriguing tale.

And he was bringing up Hadassah, that is Esther, his uncle's daughter, for she had neither father nor mother. Now the young lady was beautiful of form and face, and when her father and her mother died, Mordecai took her as his own daughter. Esther 2:7 NASB

TODAY'S HEROINE:
Esther, the Queen of Understanding

The two of us are drama queens. We met as novice actresses performing in community theatre productions in our native city of Nashville, Tennessee. We love to see the drama in even the most mundane aspects of life. When together, we are quick to cry at something poignant or tender, and we are even quicker to laugh. We often laugh so hard when we're together that we keep a bottle of Motrin close by.

We each view the other as a queen among friends. We value beyond words our thirty-year friendship. With our shared history, we feel safe and cherished and excited about facing the next thirty years as best pals. One prayer we have for you is that you are able to share this study with one or more of your queen girlfriends. Hopefully you are surrounded by a bevy of faithful girlfriends as you journey through meeting our "fore-sisters" in the Word.

In God's court, queens come in all shapes, sizes, ages, and occupations. My (Bonnie's) husband Brent has always referred to our daughter Courtney as "The Queen." He simply adores her. His affection and careful involvement in her life reflects the love of God for me. As I watch Brent's love for Courtney, I am reminded that God sees me this way, as his daughter and a queen of his heart.

Queen Esther is our heroine for today's study. She is one of only two women who have an entire book in the Bible devoted to her life, the other being Ruth. Using snapshots of the brave women in our study only allows us time to focus on our favorite highlights. So let's zero in on some of Esther's strongest lessons.

The story of Esther unfolds in ten chapters like the best drama or novel. It is full of bad guys and heroes, suspense, and victory in which the good guys finally win. It is a rags-to-riches story for a beautiful orphan child.

Let's look at this story from a woman's perspective, since that is who we are. Let's put ourselves in the sandals of Esther and see if we can gain a new perspective on this daughter of God who also is our sister. She has something to tell us about what it means to survive the culture of our day; not only to survive it, but how to thrive in it, standing against ungodliness and standing for righteousness.

First let's look at the players in Esther's story.

You already know that the two of us are actors by profession. When we take on a new role, our first work is to study the character's personality and figure out what motivates her. We delve deeply into the intentions of the character in each scene in order to portray her realistically.

Using the tools of an actor discovering her character, we will look at the major players in the story of Esther one at a time and see the kind of people who surrounded our heroine. But first, we need some back story. If we get a little perspective on the history, we'll get a better idea of what is motivating the players in our drama. Esther's story is a dramatic script or textbook guide for women who seek godliness in a godless culture.

Up until today, few of the brave women in our study have enjoyed healthy relationships with the men in their lives. Most of our heroines have persevered in spite of sexual abuse or emotional neglect.

This pattern breaks in the life of Esther! Here we meet an orphaned girl, carefully mentored by her godly cousin Mordecai. She took his teaching to heart and learned to value herself as a woman. She understood her heritage as a daughter of Jehovah. Mordecai was her biggest fan, and the man who challenged her to risk everything in order to save her people from a massacre.

Their story is intertwined; their victory for the Jews, inseparable.

Almost since the beginning of time, satan has been hard at work trying to wipe the people of Israel off the map. It happened in the past and it's happening right now. Want to hazard a guess as to why? Scripture calls the Jews the "apple of God's eye." It is through father Abraham that the covenant of promise came into the world. It is through Israel that our beloved messiah has come and brings salvation. And it is there in that beautiful land where our savior will set foot again when he returns to bring all things on this earth to their glorious conclusion.

No wonder satan is ticked off. No wonder he'd like to see the Jews disappear. The best blessings the world has ever known have come through the nation of Israel.

When we draw back the curtain on the opening scenes of Esther, we see that once again, old lucifer is hard at work trying to destroy the Jews, and he is going to use a man named Haman to try to accomplish his purposes.

But wait; God has a man as well.

His name is Mordecai.

With this highly volatile backdrop in mind, let's take a look at the players one at a time.

"Yes, if you cry out for insight and raise your voice for understanding, if you seek Wisdom as for silver and search for skillful and godly Wisdom as for hidden treasures, then you will understand the reverent and worshipful fear of the Lord and find the knowledge of our omniscient God" (Prov. 2:3-5 Amplified Bible).

Esther 101: Understand From Where You've Come Read Esther 2 and let's profile Mordecai and Esther.

Mordecai

Nationality:

Place of residence:

Job description/responsibilities:

Type of company he keeps:Interests:

Level of ego:

Character description:

Not enough can be said about Mordecai's faith, integrity, and the loving treatment of his young cousin. Esther had no one but him to teach her how to value herself, how to respond to life, how to view her heritage, and how to face the challenges in her culture. His teaching equipped her to be a righteous lady of God in a treacherous land ruled by a ruthless king. An orphan child was taken in by this bold man of God and treated as God would treat her. Because she understood where she had come from and to whom she belonged, Esther was able to rise above overwhelming challenges. Everyone should be so lucky to have a cousin like Mordecai. Now let's look at our heroine, Esther.

Esther

Nationality:

Place of residence:

Job description/responsibilities:

Type of company she keeps:Interests:

Level of ego:

What others say about her:

Character description:

Early in her life, Mordecai must have "home-schooled" Esther on many topics. One important subject would be history.

What might Uncle Mordecai have taught her about the history of the Jews living in Persia?

Turn to 2 Kings 24:8-17.

Long ago, who was king in Israel?

_____

How long did he rule?

_____

Why so short a time?

_____

Who came in to destroy Jerusalem?

_____

Eleven years later, Nebuchadnezzar completed the takeover and destruction of Jerusalem. He carried the Hebrew nation into Babylonian exile. Esther knew about the years of captivity her people endured under King Nebuchadnezzar. She also would have known that Babylon was defeated and overtaken in one night by the Medo-Persians. It's fascinating to wonder if Esther heard the stories of Daniel and of his courageous life as God's man in Babylon. Perhaps his courageous choices inspired her own.

Read Isaiah 44:24-28.

What would Esther have learned about the fate of God's people?

_____

_____

Mordecai would have taught young Esther that God used King Cyrus of the Medes to release the Jews to return home to Jerusalem, where the foundation of the temple would be rebuilt.

"Know your people's story, sweet Esther," Mordecai might have said. "Four hundred years have passed since the fall of Jerusalem. Many of our people returned to the land of Israel. Now King Xerxes holds the throne here in Persia. We live here among the Persians, part of a Diaspora."

"What does that mean, cousin?"

"For now, our people are... displaced."

Might a wide-eyed young Esther have asked, "Why do we live in a place that once held our people captive? Why don't we live in the land of our forefathers?"

"Good question," Mordecai might have replied, scratching his beard.

Why do we sometimes stay in difficult places with painful memories?

_____

Can we live in a godless place and retain our godliness?

_____

Wait, isn't that exactly where we live today? We live in a rather graceless age, and as best we can, are challenged to live out a grace-filled life. This is exactly what Esther models for each and every woman today. We can live without compromise, without giving up or giving in. We can overcome unbeatable odds if we are God's lady, even in the fat middle of our own "diaspora" or displaced surroundings.

(Back to the classroom.)

"Esther."
"Yes, Cousin Mordecai?"

"Your real name, your Hebrew name, is Hadassah."

"Hadassah.... like the myrtle?"[37]

"Yes, my dear." She takes a moment to think of the beautiful myrtle trees in the poetry of her people. "I like my real name."

"So do I, my sweet, but here in Persia, you will be called Esther, named after the Persian goddess Ishtar."

"But I don't want to be named after a Persian goddess."

"I know, my dear. Please understand your Hebrew name is your true identity. But living here, in a foreign culture, we must use a name others will recognize."

"What does Esther mean?"

Smiling, loving eyes would have relished this explanation.

"Your name here in Persia means "star." God promised to bless his people and multiply us as the stars of the heavens. You are one of his stars. Never forget this. No one can take away who you are and where you have come from. So here you are, part of Israel's sky. God's beautiful star!"[38]

What one specific instruction did Mordecai give his young cousin in Esther 2:20?

_____

_____

Esther understood who she was and where she came from. She knew she was a Hebrew lady living in a foreign culture, wearing a name layered with meaning and purpose. And she obeyed Mordecai by keeping her true identity safely hidden.

Little did Esther know she would live out the prophetic meaning of her Persian name. By now, we are beginning to see what motivates and drives our characters. We see a young girl named Esther, trapped in a man's world, powerless over her destiny. We see her cousin, fearlessly defying the law of the land and refusing to bow to the king. We are about to meet a king, careless and quick to act without measuring the impact of his decisions. This king is about to be captivated by a godly woman's powerful use of true beauty.

Esther 102: Understand the True Power of Beauty

If you were playing King Xerxes, what clues in Scripture would help bring this man to life? Remember, dialogue is the key for character revelation in a good script. Watch for things our players say and you'll find clues to their personalities. Ahasuerus was his name in Hebrew. In Greek, it was Xerxes. Let's pretend you've been given the role of King Xerxes in a production titled:

I Get My Kicks from Champagne

Or

The Good, the Bad, and the Ugly
Or

You'll Do It My Way!

Based on the facts we have about him in Scripture, fill in the following outline and think about how you would portray him. Let's zoom in for a close-up.

Read Esther 1.

Xerxes

Title:

Level of authority:

Place of residence:

Level of wealth:

Job description/responsibilities:

Interests:

Type of company he keeps:Level of ego:

Insecurities:

Character description:

Xerxes, the King of Persia, was a wild man. He was a party man. He was a man who liked what he wanted and he wanted it when he liked it. Xerxes craved power. He hated to lose face in public. His ego was fragile, his style of rule, ruthless. This king was a bi-polar cocktail of trouble; one minute happy, the next on a rampage. Haman, his best friend, drinking buddy, and second in command, was cut from the same cloth.

Before going further, let's look at one of the most evil players that ever walked across the pages of history.

Move ahead now and **read Esther 3**.

Haman

Nationality:

Place of residence:

Job description/responsibilities:

Type of company he keeps:Interests:

Level of ego:

Character description:

You have just profiled the king's right-hand man. His "go-to" guy. This czar in the Persian court had King Xerxes' ear and shared his passion for all things profitable to self. Haman fed Xerxes with the oldest poison known to man: pride. Xerxes drank from this cup without restraint, as Haman continued to fill the glass.

Their union was a recipe for disaster.

The book of Esther spans the first ten years of Xerxes' reign. In the opening chapter, we find Xerxes hosting a seven-day banquet for generals, dignitaries, and politically powerful men in the land. Ignoring the fact that Persia had suffered a costly defeat on the battlefield against Greece, Xerxes was all about showing off his palace, his wine, and his women.

When it came to women, Xerxes liked "arm candy." Queen Vashti fit the bill. She was a physical beauty—a knockout. But evidently she didn't share Xerxes' ostentatious nature. While Xerxes partied down with Haman by his side, Vashti held a separate dinner party for the visiting women. After days of drinking and sharing war stories, Xerxes sent for Vashti to come join the men. He wanted to show off his queen. Some commentaries suggest he may even have wanted her to come dressed provocatively or in the nude.

Vashti flatly refused. Xerxes immediately lost face. The Persian king cannot control his queen. Who wears the robe in this family? Somebody had to pay. Let Vashti be the one. In short order, the queen is removed. By chapter 2, she's gone from biblical history. And to make sure Vashti hasn't upset the applecart in every man's home, Xerxes sent out a royal order: All wives in Persia were to take note of what happened to Vashti. Women were commanded to jump when their husbands snapped their fingers or else they might share a similar fate.

Yet as the years passed it didn't take long for Xerxes to miss his queen. He was grumpy, angry that he'd lost too many battles, and his male ego was bruised. He was lonely and after five years wanted some new arm candy. What's a lonely, crazy king to do?

Hold a national beauty contest to find a new queen!

Let's enter the next pivotal scene with open eyes.

Read Esther 2:8-12.

Where was Esther taken?

_____

Who was with her?

_____

What process was going on?

_____

Who did she impress, according to **verse 9**?

_____

Who kept a watchful eye on her?

_____

A Persian version of *The Bachelorette* was in full swing. The young maidens spent a year of preparation. They were given spa treatments, fed a special diet, groomed for one all-important date with the king. Here we find Esther listening, watching, remembering her history, wondering what her fate would be. Hegai found Esther to be a special standout, intelligent and much more than just a physical beauty. He gave her specific instructions, special food, and choice advice.

Mordecai, an attendant in the king's court, checked in every day to see how his precious, adopted daughter was faring. Would the groundwork laid in her heart give her strength during the dark nights as she prepared for her night with the king? Everyone knew the stakes were high. The king was looking for just the right queen to replace Vashti. Any one of the young maidens who didn't measure up would be dismissed into his harem, unable to marry. In ancient times, concubines were the equivalent of slaves.

If the king never called for them again, they were destined to live as widows. This was not what Mordecai dreamed of for his Hadassah child.

"What will I do if I am chosen to stay with the king?" she might have asked her trusted cousin.

"You will do what God gives you the strength to do."

"What if he's cruel? I'm scared."

"There is no fear when Jehovah God has you in his hands. He will see and protect your every move. Trust him, Hadassah. We have no way of knowing his plans and ways. It's only for us to choose trust."

"In the eyes of our people, I will be living a life of shame...."

"Trust God, Esther. Time will tell us of his plans."

Esther understood the power of a woman's physical beauty. Most importantly, she understood that beauty might open a door, but it was how she walked through it that would shape her destiny.

She showed great wisdom when it was time for her night with Xerxes. From her cousin Mordecai, she had learned the value of listening to wise men. Before seeing the king, each girl could choose anything they wanted from the harem to take with them. Hegai advised Esther to be frugal. She took nothing with her to meet the king.

In **Esther 2:15**, how is she dscribed?

_____

_____

Esther won favor in the sight of all who saw her.

What happens in **verse 17**?

_____

Little orphan Esther is now Queen of Persia. Xerxes, the man of excess, was drawn to a woman who asked for nothing. She didn't need his approval. She knew who she was. Esther was free to be herself, to be charming, lovely, and filled with wisdom. Because of her self-assurance, she required nothing from anyone around her. For a king who lived a life of too much, he found this young maiden of confident beauty irresistible.

What does she teach us about how to live in our culture of excess?

_____

How attractive are needy people?

_____

Esther 103: Understanding Honor

Though she was now married to the most powerful king in the known world, Esther never forgot the man who acted as her father and loved her. She kept open communication with Mordecai and honored his ongoing instructions.

Take a moment to think of someone in your life whose advice helped keep you grounded when your circumstances made no sense. Write their name or initials and one or two adjectives that describe what they mean to you:

_____

_____

_____

Esther's circumstances drastically changed, but they didn't change her. She was under the thumb of a madman who had crowned her queen. Under her royal dress beat the heart of a woman who honored God above any earthly king. Esther had no identity crisis. Esther's faith in God gave her the strength to rise above the rules of a pagan marriage.

Xerxes may have crowned her queen for the day, but Esther would have been more than aware that the king had a harem of other women at his disposal every night. Movies have been made in an attempt to romanticize the relationship between Xerxes and Esther. But any woman in her situation would have little in common with a man like the king of Persia. Esther was a woman of godly honor forced into the bed of a dictator. One of the most profound attributes of her character is that she retained a sense of self-respect in such a demeaning scenario. Her self-worth was based on God's love for her. Grounded in Him, she was able to maintain her own sense of value while trapped in a dangerous marriage.

Biblical history doesn't paint Esther as an abused wife. But is there a case to be made for this argument? Explain:

_____

_____

_____

Was this Esther's dream of marriage? When she was a young girl growing up in Mordecai's home, what were her fantasies of her future husband? It is certain that she must have talked with Mordecai about the marriage he would one day arrange for her. It would be with another proper Jewish boy from a decent family in the neighborhood. This man would be hand-picked by her loving cousin. It would certainly not be a random choice made hastily or without much thought and concern.

Instead she had been forcibly taken from the only home she knew and from her only living relative. She had been chosen to be the wife of an uncircumcised pagan king who was most certainly not the virgin she was. She was relegated to the harem and surrounded only by other women and eunuchs. She could not see Mordecai when she wanted and was completely cut off from her old neighborhood and her Jewish friends. As far as we're concerned, the only perks in her life were the clothes and the endless access to the spa.

Esther honored God while enduring unthinkable circumstances. A spa can be a prison. Ever think that through? Money doesn't ensure happiness. Even in a royal palace, Esther chose to remember her God and to stay close to the wise counsel of Mordecai.

By following the destiny God marked out for her, Esther had to adjust her expectations of what life was going to "look like." If she longed for intimate conversations each day with a husband who worshiped Yahweh and who loved her for who she was, it was never going to happen. She would never have the joy of growing old with a man who wanted her and her alone.

Biblical history doesn't paint Esther as a woman who understood grief. Yet let's explore these possibilities.

It is likely that Esther had to grieve her losses. She was certainly no stranger to this process. She already had experience grieving the loss of her parents. She must now grieve the loss of dreams of an intimate marriage relationship.

This seems so unfair.

Our destiny with God is not always clear when we're walking down the paths of injustice. But he has a plan.

Is there anything about her story that resonates with yours?

_____

_____

_____

Are there dreams and plans you've had to release?

_____

_____

Has life turned out differently than what you expected?

_____

_____

Welcome to the human race.

Like Esther, we feel anger and deep disappointment with the way some things in our lives turn out. This is true for everyone at some point.

The biggest question is: How do we handle our heartache? Where do we take it?

_____

_____

We are wise to make a habit of taking our brokenness to the only one who can give on-going comfort and the healing we deeply desire. We have a son of man and son of God who walked this messy planet and saw first-hand how lives are upended by circumstances out of their control. God had something in mind for Esther that she couldn't see. His purposes for her unfolded one day at a time and often were confusing. Sound familiar? Her life is not different from ours in this regard. She had to walk by faith, and so do we. She had to trust the final outcome to God. So do we.

There are answers to questions that eventually will come in this life, and some questions that will remain unanswered until we're face-to-face with Jesus. That's just life in a fallen world. And that's what our faith walk is all about: Going forward without all the answers. Going forward certain that the steadfast loving kindness of our father never fails.

One day we will live out the answers to our questions.

Until then, we have a savior who sits at the right hand of God and intercedes for us in our weak attempts to make sense of life in this fallen garden.

For Esther, the hope we have in Christ was represented by the presence and influence of Mordecai in her life.

Even if Esther got the big picture and later understood that she had been providentially placed in the kingdom and used mightily by God to save the entire Jewish population in Persia, it would have been understandable for her to wish God had chosen someone else to fulfill his purposes. Yet Mordecai had taught Esther that God's delivering hand was always on the move. Still, it's human nature to think, *God won't use me!* Or, *God, please don't entrust this to my hands!* It would have been natural for Esther to have wished God had chosen some other way.

Turn for a minute and note the following response to God's call to action:

In Exodus 4:10, what did Moses say to the Lord?

_____

_____

The Amplified Bible reads, "I am not eloquent or a man of words, neither before nor since You have spoken to Your servant; for I am slow of speech and have a heavy and awkward tongue." Does this protest bring a smile to your face? Don't you love it? Moses was trying so hard to convince the maker of his body that his body wasn't up for the task. God is the most affirming parental presence in our lives. He believes more in who we are than we do. He sees beyond where we are and into who we'll be. In the end, Moses finds the courage to confront Pharaoh and lead a nation through a wilderness. He talks as God's friend, face-to-face. From a stuttering, fearful step of faith, he strides into biblical history as a foreshadowing figure of Jesus.

In Jonah 4:2-3, we find one of the more humorous responses to the call of God. Read those verses and describe this reluctant prophet's mood:

_____

In **Jonah 3:6,** Jonah's message came across loud and clear. The king of Nineveh humbled himself and called his nation to repent after Jonah's powerful proclamation from the Lord. Then watching God's mercy fall on Israel's enemies was the last straw. Jonah threw a temper tantrum and demanded that God kill them! You've got to love Jonah.

The Lord uses whomever, whenever and however he pleases to take his love to the world. Even the stumbling, doubting, weak, and worn are never wasted in his hands. His son knew well how the call of God can seem to be far too much to bear.

Jesus certainly asked the father to find some other way than using his life on a cross to redeem the human race. "Let this cup pass from me… nevertheless…." In this prayer, Jesus gave credibility to our own protests and pleas when we hit the crossroads in our lives, and feel inadequate for the task.

Christ knows the ache of lost dreams. He longed to take Jerusalem under his care, but was rejected by his own. He wept over a best friend's death even though he knew Lazarus would be raised back to life. He was moved at every turn to touch those who hurt, because he walked through our messy world. Because he understands, he went to the cross to deliver us from the injustices of this world. In the face of Jesus, our disappointments meet his tender eyes of compassion.

Do you feel your hopes and dreams have been hijacked at certain points along the way?

_____

Then you and Esther have more in common than you know. She too may have felt like a hijacked queen. Esther also may have suffered the separation from Mordecai as one of the most painful losses in her new role in Persian royalty. But God's providence placed Mordecai in a pivotal position. Like Esther, God puts people in our lives along the way to encourage us to keep on keeping on.

Read Esther 2:21-23.

Where was Mordecai stationed?

_____

Mordecai worked at the king's gate. This gave him access to all manner of political information.

What did he make known to Esther?

_____

Where were these events recorded?

_____

Doing the right thing always is the wise choice. Mordecai chose to be God's man in a foreign environment. Little did he know how his choices would affect the life of Esther and the future of their people.

TODAY'S DATE: _____

YOUR HEADLINE:

_____

"Knowing what is right is like deep water in the heart; a wise person draws from the well within" (Prov. 20:5 The Message).

Week Eleven
BREAKING NEWS

The Persian Pulse

ESTROGEN SURGE TOPPLES TRAITOR, SAVES NATION

The Persian Pulse recently broke the news about the execution of Haman, Persia's chief advisor to King Xerxes I. The story continues with recent updates; it appears Queen Esther, the winner of *Bachelorette Season 496 B. C.*, has been working behind the scenes. Both clever and beautiful, inside sources report that she may well have been the one who inspired the radical turn of events, in which Jews have been given permission to arm themselves against unprovoked attacks. The Queen hosted two intimate dinner parties over the past week for the king and Haman. Persia's Pompous Catering Cartel reported both Xerxes and his top advisor were getting along splendidly until late into the second afternoon.

One of the servers spoke off the record. "I was serving the wine, and in and out of the room, so I don't know the whole story…. But I can tell you this: King Xerxes left the first dinner party complaining about how he wasn't tired and didn't know if he could get to sleep. For Haman, it went downhill from there."

A spokesman from The Library of Persian History was summoned to read Xerxes a bedtime story. "About halfway through recalling the defeat of the Spartan leader Leonidus, the king seemed to smile and nod off," said the source, who wished to remain anonymous. I had just recounted his order to behead the Spartan warrior and have his body placed on a pole for public display. But when I moved ahead to the story of Mordecai, suddenly Xerxes shot straight up out of bed. He realized Mordecai had never been honored for saving the king's life."

Only recently, **The Persian Pulse** covered the story of Mordecai's honored ceremony, dressed in the royal robes of Xerxes and riding the king's horse. A body language expert described Haman as "tensely reluctant" as he led Mordecai through the city streets. One man standing near the edge of the parade noted, "Haman was shouting, 'This is a man the king delights to honor.' But then I swear I heard him mutter under his breath, "But not for long!"

Neighbors of Haman describe hearing a lot of hammering and seeing lumber brought in only days before the parade. Oddly, Haman was executed at his own construction site.

His wife Zeresh went on record saying, "Haman was bi-polar and given to fits of rage. But not even I would have dreamed he was capable of murder." Asked about the bizarre construction near her home, she simply added, "We've always talked about adding on a great room." Word on the street is that the King has put out an arrest warrant for Haman's ten sons.

Jews have been rejoicing in the streets with cheering, cries of joy, and prayers to their God. News of the king's new proclamation is spreading through the Persian hillsides like wildfire.

By order of Queen Esther, the fourteenth and fifteenth Days of Adar will now and forever be a holiday for all Jews. It shall be called The Feast Of Purim (meaning, a "roll of the dice.") In a country that loves a good party, this promises to be one for the history books.

Editor's note: Any opinions expressed about the Jews do not necessarily reflect the view of *The Persian Pulse*.)

But Mordecai found out about the plot and told Queen Esther, who in turn reported it to the king, giving credit to Mordecai. Esther 2:22 NIV

TODAY'S HEROINE:
Esther, part two

Esther 104: Understanding Your Enemy

Esther has much to teach us about good versus evil. We live in culture that wants to blur the lines. It's not popular, even in many churches, to talk about sin. We hear a lot about "poor choices," "owning your life," and "finding your center of spirituality." The refusal to acknowledge sin is spitting in the face of Jesus on the cross. If there are no real enemies of God, then why was it necessary for the son of God to die?

Read Romans 3:10-12.

Who is righteous?

_____

Who seeks after God?

_____

None. Not one of us, no matter how much good we try to do, all our works are as filthy rags when we use them to try to justify us before God. None can earn grace. The wonder of God's great love is that it is a gift freely given. To those who believe in the work of Jesus on the cross and in his resurrected power, we are given the grace to live out lives of gratitude for God's mercy.

Read Ephesians 2:8 for a little spa moment for your soul.

Is this verse a stress reliever? Why?

_____

_____

When we were dead and hopelessly lost, God saved us. Any cultural perspective that attempts to diminish the evil of satan is a perspective steeped in self-achievement.

Bob Dylan penned a brilliant song called *Ring Them Bells*. The last lines of the song describe the battle that has raged since Eden:

"For the lines are long
And the fighting is strong.
And they're breaking down the distance between right and wrong."

We have an enemy. Wise women are awake to the spiritual battles we fight in prayer.

What does **John 10:10** teach us?

_____

Jesus came to give us life in all its fullness. But there is a parallel plan going on all around us to steal, devour, and destroy. Esther did not back away from the enemy of her people. She assessed the situation and with clear understanding waited for God's direction, determined to fight back.

Mordecai's messages alerted Queen Esther about the dangerous edicts emerging from Xerxes' court. Haman, a descendant of Israel's enemies (an Agagite from the line of Esau) hated the Jews. For generations his family told stories of King Saul and how Israel had destroyed their nation. **(See 1 Samuel 15 for this back story**.) We discover that in Esther's lifetime the centuries-old hatred hit a raging peak. Out of this need for revenge Haman adopted a powerful political agenda. He had a one-track mind with one purpose and one goal: **Exterminate the Jews in Persia.**

This message was on Haman's BlackBerry and written in bold ink at the top of each day on his calendar. It was the primary application on his iPhone and etched into the darkness of his heart. He had put in motion the time and place when every despised Jew would at last be slaughtered. He convinced Xerxes to use his royal seal when sending out the order. **Their nation would be destroyed during Passover.**

More than anyone, Haman wanted to kill Mordecai.

Turn to Esther 4:1-3.

As a Hebrew representative at the city gate, how did Mordecai respond to this news?

_____

_____

In **verse 8,** what does Esther receive?

_____

Her hour has arrived. She has choices to make.

Esther 105: Understanding Your Hour

Esther's hour in history is now ticking loudly in her spirit, minute by minute without a moment to spare. She has to make the biggest decision of her life. Every question about why an orphaned Hebrew girl would become Queen of Persia now comes into extreme focus.

Mordecai has commissioned her to approach the king on their behalf and to save her people.

Her initial reply rips at our hearts. It's as if she is once again a little girl needing her trusted guardian's best advice.

"How can I go to the king? It's been over thirty days since he asked for me."

"Yes, Hadassah, I know. But you must try."

"His moods are unpredictable....   I don't have a clue what he has been up to...."

"He's been plotting with Haman to wipe out our people."

"If I go at the wrong time he could have me executed on the spot. He doesn't even know who I am! He doesn't know that I'm a Jew!"

"It wasn't the right time to tell him before. Now is the time. Now is your hour."

The end of Esther 4 is most often quoted and remembered.

Read verses 13-14.

Do you find anything new in this famous passage?

_____

Esther Master Class: Taking On Your Hour Understand That If You Stand Down, Another Will Take Your Place

We often quote Mordecai's observation that Esther was born for "such a time as this." And so she was. So are we all. Each of us has been intentionally placed into our culture, our family, our lifetime by God for his purposes.

Turn and read Ephesians 2:10 and Acts 17:26.

Take a moment to look around you. Have you ever considered that you were knit in your mothers' womb to live exactly in this century? You were placed here before the foundations of the earth to be who you are, where you are, and on God's timetable to live out good works specifically designed for you!

What does this mean for you today?

_____

_____

_____

_____

Mordecai told Esther it was time to step out and believe God had allowed her to be in a pivotal position in Persia's royal palace for exactly this moment: her moment. Personally, the most striking part of his bold statement is when he says:

"If you keep silent at this time, relief and deliverance shall arise for the Jews from elsewhere, but you and your father's house will perish" (Amplified Bible).

God will accomplish his will. We can either cooperate and believe him or someone else will be used in our place. For those of us who take God at his word, we are convinced that nothing will ever separate us from his love. We read over and over again of how we are his and called by Christ to be his testimony.

But what if Esther had backed away? She had every right to be terrified at the thought of approaching the king and revealing her identity. If she survived the initial encounter, she would then face the daunting challenge of asking Xerxes to spare the lives of her people. Her hesitation is brief, but completely understandable.

We all have chances to believe in a huge God with a huge plan for our lives. Yet God, ever the gentleman, never forces our free will in the process.

Mordecai bluntly informed Esther that she had a choice. But if she didn't rise to this hour, God would deliver his people through another means. And in the process, did she think by avoiding her hour she would save her life? No chance.

Life would go on without her, without her family. But it would go on. Why? **Because God's covenant to his people is irrevocable. She had learned this truth as a young girl at Mordecai's knee.**

PRAY UP BEFORE STEPPING OUT

Esther's statement in 4:16 shows us that she came to a place of peace about her destiny. Remember how we said that dialogue in a good script reveals the heart of the character? This verse stands out above them all when it comes to Esther's character revelation.

"If I perish, I perish" (NIV).

Write in your own words what Esther was saying in this phrase.

_____

_____

Can you remember a time in your own life when you came to a crossroads that demanded your total commitment no matter the personal cost? Briefly describe it.

_____

_____

_____

Esther determined to face her hour swiftly, decisively, and without turning back.

She was a diligent student. Her heart was filled with stories of God's faithfulness. He had parted seas and fed his people in the wilderness. And didn't Mordecai tell her over and over again that God promised to bless those who blessed Israel, and curse those who cursed them?

From **Esther 4:15-17 and into 5:1**, describe Esther's preparation for battle.

_____

_____

Decide. Pray. Fast. Surround yourself with a posse of praying people. Take the risk no matter the outcome. Think through the coming battle. Prepare and trust. Move onto the battlefield.

In **chapters 5 and 6** we read of Esther's brilliant strategic moves on the battlefield of the palace. She finds favor with Xerxes, who seems grateful for her company.

From the royal throne room to the dining room, Esther times each move with precision. She knows that Haman is a loose cannon. He must be kept close and included in her plan of attack.

She has given God ample room to bless each choice, having first prayed for his covering.

Our next scene in this unfolding drama calls for an elaborate set and a gorgeous costume for our heroine.

Read Esther 5.

According to **Esther 5:1**, how is she dressed when she approaches the king?

_____

_____

How did the king show a favorable attitude toward her, according to **verses 2-7**?

_____

_____

This grandiose offer was used frequently in ancient times by rulers in power. A more modern translation might be, "Esther, you rock, babe! You are my rock star! What can I do

133

to make you truly happy? You name it and it's yours. Here's my American Express Platinum Credit Card. Go for it."

Esther once more carefully measures her requests. We are reminded of how she came into Xerxes' presence asking for nothing. She was not a needy queen. She asks now only for the honor of hosting two dinner parties for the king and his right-hand man.

Why do you think Esther waited another day before telling Xerxes what was on her mind?

_____

_____

We only can speculate as to her reasons for doing this, but it's interesting to see the progression of events that are allowed to occur because of her delay.

Turn to the final verses of Esther 5.

The first party goes well. Haman is all over this, heady and prideful. He's part of the elite crowd. Only Xerxes, Esther, himself, and the palace chefs. What a coup.

What does Haman do after his intimate dinner with royalty?

_____

_____

What does he call Mordecai in **verse 13**?

_____

On his way home after the initial dinner party he sees Mordecai. And what a party pooper he is. Mordecai is a constant thorn in Haman's side. He simply will not bow, he will not drink the Kool-Aid, this impetuous Jew. Haman's anti-Semitism is being allowed to ripen. In God's timing, the evil thing still has to progress a little more before God steps in to answer it. Esther doesn't know this yet. Whatever her personal reasons for delaying her request, God used them for his purposes. As the night wore on, Haman's anger simmered to a boil. At home, he ranted and raved and then his wife made a bold suggestion.

How did Zeresh stoke the fires of hatred in her husband's heart? **See Esther 5:14.**

_____

How did this idea go over with Haman?

_____

Need we say more? He was delighted, comforted, even energized about building a gallows on which to hang Mordecai. In fact this was such a brilliant idea that perhaps he should request Xerxes act on this execution as soon as possible. Heady with revenge, Haman headed back to the palace.

Oh, but Xerxes was having a restless night. The king couldn't sleep. Maybe if someone read from the chronicles of Persian history it would work like a sedative. Especially if they skipped past the part where he had entire armies impaled just for fun. That part was a bit too exciting.

In Esther 6, every plan of the enemy begins to backfire.

What did Esther's delay allow the king to do?

_____

Even though the book of Esther never names the name of God, it is obvious that his hand is all over it. Ever wonder why you can't go to sleep at times? Maybe it's not because of too much caffeine. Maybe it's a greater purpose of God at work in your life!

It was no accident that Xerxes could not sleep. It was no accident that he asked for the record of his reign to be read to him. And it was no accident that the attendant turned to a passage written five years earlier about the honorable deeds of a man named Mordecai.

Before going further, let's look closely at the implications of God's timing versus our own. For five years Mordecai's loyalty was overlooked. Until this night, this all-important night in the history of the Jews, when a sleepless king's memory was awakened.

How does this make you feel? Have the events of your life felt random at times? Have you ever felt the shaping of your destiny was something God left to chance?

_____

_____

INHALE/EXHALE TIME! Let's stop for a moment, like Queen Esther, and have our own version of a banquet. There are hundreds of passages in Scripture that show us the sovereignty of God and his deliberate attention to the details in our lives.

What does **Ephesians 1:11** tell us?

_____

God works out everything in conformity with the purpose of his will. That's not just a few things, but everything. In every detail of your life, he is working to fulfill the purpose for your life.

If he knows when a sparrow falls, and the hairs of our head are numbered, then it is safe to assume he is into the details of all that concerns us. Every time we shampoo or brush our hair, the number of hairs on our heads changes. So God must be into a daily head count! If he knows the number of hairs on our head on any given day, then we can rest assured he cares about the big stuff too.

For more spa moments for your soul, here are some glorious passages that are guaranteed to build your faith and give you peace about God's involvement in your life and how things are going to turn out for you. Pick out one of the following verses and write it below. Then memorize it so you can recall it in bed at night when you feel fear creeping in and robbing you of peace.

Ephesians 1:11; Romans 11:36; Romans 8:28; Psalm 33:10-12; Proverbs 16: 1, 9; Acts 17: 46; Isaiah 46:10.

_____

_____

God always is at work, even during the pauses… or when we feel we're on "hold." While Esther was summoning up her courage and planning another banquet for her husband and the man who had issued her death warrant, God was about the business of being sovereign and working all things into conformity with his will.

What ironic twist happens to Haman in **Esther 6:4-14**?

_____

_____

Can you imagine how Haman felt? A ton of nasty adjectives jump quickly to our minds. Haman went to the palace that evening certain he could convince the king to kill Mordecai. Just a few verses later, he found himself in the unthinkable position of honoring the man he wanted dead. In a royal public display, detailed by his own words, Haman was forced to parade Mordecai around the city dressed in Xerxes' finest robes while riding the king's horse. And through clenched teeth and a forced smile, Haman was commanded to say what in **verse 11?**

_____

_____

We almost can feel Haman's blood pressure rising with rage. His hatred of Mordecai and every Jew in the kingdom is now at a fevered pitch. He returns home and this time his wife makes things worse. She reminds Haman that Mordecai is a Jew. Jews seem to have something going on that no one else understands. How can Haman possibly win?

Ever wonder what must have been going through Mordecai's mind? For the past weeks, he has lived with the horror of knowing his death sentence had been signed and sealed by the king himself. Now, in a classic reversal of destiny, Mordecai is paraded through the streets of Persia as a man on the receiving end of the king's highest honor.

Mordecai is not overly impressed with the honor or with himself. After the parade, Mordecai has a polar opposite heart response from that of Haman. There is no bragging or assumption. Mordecai simply goes back to work, faithful in what he has been called to do. He doesn't relax and say, "Well I guess the worst is over. I'm in! And if the king goes ahead and annihilates the Jews, I guess he won't kill me now that he remembers I saved his life!"

Mordecai remains God-focused. He will not rest until he sees the deliverance of his people.

Read Esther 7 and 8. <u>Trust the timing of God. The right moment will come. When it comes, take it!</u>

The second dinner party runs a little less smoothly than the first. Esther is again given access to the AMEX card in **Esther 7:2**. Xerxes must wonder what is on her mind. The time is ripe. Our heroine must now face her fear and confront the king with the truth. She not only reveals Haman's plot to murder all the Jews in the kingdom, but also reveals her own nationality. She confesses to being a Jew. She aligns herself with the condemned.

Read 7:3-6.

How does Esther word her request?

_____

_____

"If I have found favor
If it pleases the king
let my life be given me as my petition, and my people as my request" (NKJV).

Esther kept her cool. She had prepared for this very moment with the king. She knew his ego would respond to a submissive approach. Without rushing ahead of herself, she allowed Xerxes to ask the questions. As she explains that she and her people face extermination, the king is enraged.

What does he ask? **See verse 5.**

_____

_____

How does Esther answer?

_____

_____

Of course, what she doesn't say to her husband the king is equally important as what she reveals. She doesn't say, "And oh, by the way, may I point out that you're the doofus who signed this thing into reality? While you were carelessly handing off your signet ring, you happened to overlook the fact that Haman was busy plotting the murder of innocent people. I thought you were the king! What were you thinking?"

Esther doesn't revile or criticize Xerxes' lack of kingly wisdom. She humbles herself before him. Of all the lessons Esther brings to us, this may be the most difficult to apply to our own lives. Many times we are forced to deal with unreasonable or irrational people. Sometimes these folks are our employers. Sometimes we are married to them, or they are our friends. We are faced with the difficult task of working with them, living with them, dealing with their demands or tantrums or cruelty.

Esther remained humble and calm while in the company of dangerous people. We can learn from her example that staying in the place of humble obedience before God, trusting him to have the final word in our lives is more important than lashing back at people who treat us unfairly. She understood that vengeance belonged to God. Her faith was well-founded. God did not let her down. He came through for her and for the entire Jewish population in Persia.

Now read 7:7-10.

What goes around comes around. The light of truth breaks apart the lies of darkness. Haman completely comes undone. Without vitriol or melodrama, Esther brilliantly allows truth to turn the spotlight on the two men center stage. The king leaves the dining room to collect his thoughts. After all, he is the King of Persia, and has unknowingly signed Esther's death warrant.

Verse 8 is packed with drama. Describe the scene in which Xerxes returns to the room:

_____

_____

Haman appears to be making sexual advances on Queen Esther. What a perfectly timed error. Now Xerxes has legal grounds for treason and an immediate call for Haman's execution.

What happens to God's enemy?

_____

_____

"Never once in all of Haman's peacock strutting and evil plotting had God ignored him or his plans to murder Mordecai and the Jews. God had not missed his statements, the pride of his heart, the violent and prejudicial motives behind his decisions. God was invisible, but He was not out of touch or passive. He had not forgotten his people or his promises to them—and to their enemies." [39]

Take a moment to speak this truth into your heart. God has not forgotten me! Speak this into the places where you feel God is silent and doesn't see your pain, the places where you wonder if God has turned his back on your dreams or your family. Remember that he is ever-present. He is El Roi, the God who sees. He looks into every man's heart. And he is ever working on our behalf to bring beauty from ashes.

Write the current cry of your heart to him, full of praise and intimacy:

_____

_____

_____

As the book of Esther continues, please enjoy reading of how Xerxes honored both his queen and her cousin Mordecai in allowing them to reverse his own official orders of extermination.

Here are few highlights of this victory.

In **Esther 8:1-2**, what happens?

_____

Esther and Mordecai need no longer live in fear, hiding their Hebrew nationality from the Persian government. Zeresh is given packing orders and soon there's a warrant out to execute Haman's ten sons.

God indeed has the final word. As Haman and his sons hung from the seventy-five foot gallows for all of Susa to see, Esther could rejoice in knowing that evil had been conquered. The lies were uncovered. Truth was revealed and justice prevailed. God had once again kept his promise to "curse him who curses you" (Gen. 12:1-3 NKJV).

In **Esther 8:8, 11** what stunning privileges are given?

_____

_____

Esther's Legacy: The Feast Of Purim

Read Esther 9 and 10.

What holiday did Esther put into writing?

_____

How long was this holiday to be observed?

_____

There were 100 million people living in the Persian Empire. Fifteen million of them were Jews. As the curtain closes on this beautiful drama, we see Esther and Mordecai making sure that not only the Jews living in Persia at the time, but also all Jews in succeeding generations would remember the days during the reign of King Xerxes when God delivered them from the evil plot of Haman and his plan for their extermination.

"If this official celebration of Purim had not been established, what happened during Esther's lifetime would have been forgotten within two or three generations," writes Charles Swindoll. "That's why it is so important to celebrate.

This is the only book the Jews can turn to and find roots for their holiday of Purim. To this day, when they read from the scrolls of Esther, little children come dressed in costumes and adults dress up as well. The atmosphere is like an old-time melodrama. Everyone cheers the hero and heroine (Mordecai and Esther) and they boo, hiss and stomp their feet when the name of Haman is reenacted. It's a reenactment of triumph. And that's exactly how God planned it." [40]

Over the centuries, Jews have pulled out the story of Esther to give them hope in troubled times. During the Holocaust they would remind themselves of God's mighty deliverance of the displaced Hebrews in Persia. For many, this must have been especially bittersweet when no one like Esther rose up from the highest ranks of German's evil military machine.

Yet there are countless stories of people like Esther who risked everything in an attempt to save the Jewish people. There are thrilling stories of the underground movement and how men, women, and children were smuggled out of the danger and into safety.

At the close of World War II, there was a rebirth of the nation of Israel in 1948. After centuries of exile, millions of Jews returned to live in the Holy Land. We are wise to remember God's unchanging covenant with his people and to pray for peace in their land.

Through the centuries, this story continues to be told. In this special Feast of Purim celebrated every year, the Jewish people feast and give each other gifts. They tell their children about the courage of Queen Esther and how God used her to deliver their people.

Like Esther, we are orphaned children, welcomed into the arms of a loving father. We have been grafted into the line of Abraham by faith in our Jewish savior, Jesus Christ. Yet none of us need live with an orphan mentality. Following Esther's example we can understand who we are, where we came from, and how to live as honorable women no matter what we face. Like her, we look for our time and hour, open to any opportunity to deliver Good News to this generation.

As we close, let's look at a timeline of the events of this story. In 483 B. C. , Vashti was deposed as queen. In 479 B. C. , Esther was chosen to replace her. In 475 B. C. , Haman's plot to exterminate the Jews was revealed and Esther interceded for her people. Just eleven years later, in 464 B. C. , Xerxes was assassinated and his son Artaxerxes took over the throne. Artaxerxes's mother was Vashti. The history books tell us that Vashti had great influence over her son as he reigned. It seems certain she would have moved back into the palace.

Artaxerxes ruled for 39 years.

What happened to Esther? Was she relegated to some dark corner of the harem? When her husband Xerxes was killed, she was probably in her early thirties. Where did she go? How long did Mordecai live? Did the two of them make a safe exit from the Persian stage and back to the land of Israel?

What would be your favorite scenario for Esther if we had chapters 11, 12, or 13?

_____

_____

Did she look back and wonder if it was worth it? Did she continue to mourn her losses? These are questions we'll ask her in heaven. Until then, we have to remember she was just like us. She was a woman. She had dreams and hopes, laughter, and heartache. She had good days and bad days. She had hormones. And if she lived long enough, she had hot flashes. We can be certain that through it all, Esther kept the faith and completed the work God had planned for her since before he made the world.

The history of God's people is one of unpredictable adventure. No one who follows him will ever find life boring. Queen Esther's story is drenched with drama. Daughters of God are constantly being challenged and renewed. The Lord delights us with his invitation to join him on an eternal path of discovery. His ways are unknowable. We breathlessly walk on, trusting him, ever astonished by his amazing grace and how it runs through the lives of his people like a rushing river.

That's all he calls any of us to do. And he asks us to trust him in the middle of circumstances that feel crazy and out of control. Those circumstances alternately feel frightening, exhilarating, glorious, victorious, and lonely.

A. B. Simpson, founder of the Christian and Missionary Alliance, said, "God is preparing his heroes and when the opportunity comes, he can fit them into their places in a moment, and the world will wonder where they came from." This certainly describes Esther. She came out of nowhere and became queen of the civilized world. Esther takes her place alongside Joseph and Daniel as servants of God who were prepared by God, and when the time came, they stepped forward and fulfilled the calling on their lives in a pagan society.

This also is true for us. Most of us will never be called on to do something as public as Esther's ministry. We find ourselves stepping forward in other ways, most of them quiet and unseen.

Can you name one place where you are stepping forward in your day?

_____

We are chosen and prepared by God to live these days in bold and glorious faith. We are called to stand. Sometimes, great risk is involved by our choices. We trust the outcome to God.

At the end of it, we'll see victory and there will be much worth celebrating. This is our time. Oh, beloved, with rich understanding and trust in Christ, let us embrace the hour!

TODAY'S DATE: _____

YOUR HEADLINE:

_____

"To thy grace and the care of thy covenant
I commit myself, in sickness and in health,
for thou hast overcome the world,
fulfilled the law,
finished justifying righteousness,
swallowed up death in victory,
and taken all power everywhere." [41]

Palm of Deborah Fan Club

Judge, Mother, Prophetess, Commander-In-Chief, Wife, Singer/Songwriter, Motivational Speaker to host PRAISE SERVICE TODAY!

We are thrilled to announce that the nation of Israel will host a Praise and Worship Service today at Judge Deborah's Palm Tree Court in Ephraim. Opening the service, the judge will sing an original song written to honor the Lord's victorious campaign and defeat of Sisera's army. General Barak will join her in singing the duet.

Deborah's website post reads: ***"My heart goes out to the commanders of Israel who offered themselves willingly among the people. Bless the Lord!"***

Attendance is expected to be overwhelming as the nation comes together to hear this amazing mother of Israel sing a song of victory. Our many years of suffering have ended. God heard our cries and through the wise strategic leadership of Deborah, Jabin's troops have been completely destroyed.

Lappidoth, the proud husband of Judge Deborah and longtime supporter of his talented wife and their children, will be in attendance with her at the event. Deborah's rule in Israel has inspired our military leaders and the nation at large to stand up and follow Jehovah as revival sweeps the land.

Proof that there are no glass ceilings with God, Judge Deborah will no doubt go down in history as a woman unhindered by stereotypes. As a queen of multitasking, Deborah leads with a rare combination of humility and boldness.

FEMALE JUDGE PACKS HEAT

Thanks to her inspiration on the battlefield, Barak and his men fought bravely as God went before them to deliver a total victory over Israel's enemies. Crediting God as her source of power, Judge Deborah has put our country back on course.

Sharing the stage today will be another brave woman, Jael, wife of Heber. Jael dealt the final death blow to Sisera in her family's tent. The unusual dynamic trio proves God can use women and men in the battle of good over evil.

Truly, today the hills of Ephraim will be alive with music as Judge Deborah and Barak lead us in praises of victory to our Jehovah Lord.

(Any and all unauthorized recordings of Deborah's song are allowed, encouraged, and will not be punishable by law.)

Look at what you were when God called you. Not many of you were wise in the way the world judges wisdom. Not many of you had great influence. Not many of you came from important families. But God chose the foolish things of the world to shame the wise, and he chose the weak things of the world to shame the strong. 1 Cor. 1:26-27 New Century Version

TODAY'S HEROINE:
Deborah, judge and mother of Israel

Over the past 100 years, many battles have been fought in the name of women's rights. In the early 1900s, the suffragette movement resulted in giving American women the right to vote. For decades women in the United States have lobbied tirelessly for equal pay in the workplace.

Somewhere along the way, perhaps with the birth of a sexual revolution, the movement went sideways. Stay-at-home moms began to apologize and feel like they didn't "measure up." Many American women demanded the right to work and have a family too. They could do it all. Then came the demand to make choices with their bodies with birth control and the right to terminate a pregnancy. In the 1970s women insisted on the right to burn their bras and to do whatever they wanted. Before we knew it the voices of NOW (the National Organization for Women) represented women's rights in the political arena.

Women demand to be viewed as equals of men in a gender-blind society. Many continue to honorably serve in our military. Recently we witnessed the first female presidential candidate pursuing the highest office in the land. Many of these freedoms make perfect sense in a country that prides itself in giving everyone the God-given right to "life, liberty, and the pursuit of happiness."

Yet the scales of equality still tip wildly from one side to the other. The NOW movement winces when women are called the "weaker sex." But the rush for equality with men leaves both sexes caught in a politically correct identity crisis. After a century-plus of demands for respect, a strong case could be made that women are currently more disrespected than ever before in advertising, the media, and the arts. Women may lobby for choice and equality. The obvious, wonderful differences between the sexes remain and need not be at odds. Yet the enemy of God's creation continues to lie. Women are enticed to eat from the tree of self-worship and be their own god.

Thankfully, we can look to ancient biblical history and find timeless examples of women with true significance, confident and comfortable in their identity. They made no demands. Their self-worth and strength came from prayer, wisdom, faith, and a well-rounded appreciation of their womanhood. These women did not waste energy or time trying to compete with men. They lived out the beautiful plans of their lives, trusting in who God made them to be.

Deborah was one such woman. She stepped up and into "her hour" on earth with calm courage in God. She had no fear of limitations because she was a woman. Deborah saw herself made in God's image as his girl. Deborah was not a victim of womanhood. Her gender was not a barrier of weakness she had to rise above. She was a person of faith, a woman who believed God. Her role in leadership was used to display the strength of God's hand.

Jehovah's Deborah is the queen mother of women's liberation.

Both Esther and Deborah were pivotal leaders in a critical season of Israel's history. But their battlefields could have not have been more opposite. Let's look at some of the profound differences and similarities in their circumstances.

We recently learned that Esther became queen of what country?

_____

(Other than Mordecai) how would you describe the men in her world?

_____

Briefly recall where she fought her battle with King Xerxes and Haman.

_____

How did Esther prepare for battle?

_____

Queen Esther, principal wife of Xerxes, lived in a castle surrounded with spa treatments and servants. Her identity was rock-solid, and she learned from her cousin Mordecai all about how to be a wise, beautiful daughter of the living God. She used her faith-filled beauty and charm to win the respect of a dangerous king. Xerxes and his best friend were bloodthirsty, ruthless men with egos on steroids, controlling and out of control. Her battlefield was the banquet hall of a royal dining room. Her strategy was timing. She prepared for battle through fasting and prayer.

Now turn to Judges 4.

THE STATE OF DEBORAH'S STATE

Deborah's world could not have been more different than that of Queen Esther. Today's heroine lived in the time of the judges. This period of time has been called Israel's Dark Age, a time of moral and spiritual decline. Our heroine was born near the end of an eighty-year period of peace and prosperity when the land and the people of Israel had rest from her enemies. But as she grew into adulthood, old patterns had taken hold of Israel once more.

In the opening verses of Judges 4, we find a vivid picture of the political climate of her day. The first verse of Judges 4 carries a commentary repeated like a badly scratched recording throughout this period in Israel's history.

Read Judges 4:1-3.

How were God's people behaving?

_____

Who did the Lord allow to rule over them?

_____

Who was the commander of his army?

_____

How did they treat the Israelites?

_____

For how many years?

_____

What did Israel do again?

_____

Why do you think they cried out to God?

_____

Jehovah sold them into the hands of their enemies and the Israelites were severely oppressed for twenty years by the cruel reign of Jabin, King of Canaan. When we're in over our heads and the world looks like it's coming apart at the seams, our knees more easily bend. In the times when it seems that no answer comes and the enemy has more money, more power, more stamina, and more strength, we are more likely to open our mouths and cry out for help.

THINK IT THROUGH: Do you feel as though you are in a "twenty-year battle" with the enemy? If so, how?

_____

_____

How do you feel when today's equivalent of 900 chariots line up against you or someone you love?

_____

_____

Cry out to the Lord! He always is listening. He never changes, and his love for you never wavers. There are battles going on in the heavens all around you. Cry out as Israel did, never afraid to ask for help no matter how many setbacks.

What was life like during this time of oppression? We get a few clues from reading **Judges 5:6-8**. Please read those verses to see a clearer picture of the daily lives of the Israelites at this time.

What were the roads like?

_____

What did travelers have to use to get from place to place?

_____

What kind of lifestyle ceased?

_____

According to **verse 8,** what happened when the Israelites chose to worship other gods?

_____

_____

We see from these sad verses that open travel was unsafe. Enemy troops or bands of robbers made it impossible to use the roadways from one town to another. The people had to look for trails or paths through mountains or forests and travel in secret.

ISRAEL SECURITY LEVEL: RED

These verses also reveal that open life in villages was no longer possible. The people had to live in walled towns for protection from their oppressors. Gone was their freedom and safety, the enjoyment of open spaces and lovely views of the horizon. No longer could friends and neighbors linger at a well to talk with one another. They had to build fortresses around themselves to sleep in relative safety at night. Because of their idol worship and blended lifestyles with the pagan peoples around them, the Israelites had no military means to defend themselves against the Canaanites who were dominating them. The Canaanites were trying to regain their power in the Promised Land and the tribes they were oppressing were Zebulun and Naphtali. Part of the tribes of Manasseh, Issachar and Asher also were under Jabin's cruel tyranny. These were terrible times for God's chosen people.

Now read Luke 18:7.

What does God do for those who cry out to him day and night?

_____

_____

His answers appear exactly on time. They may seem to come in unlikely ways and at a snail's pace. Yet the Word tells us he will always give what is right and bring deliverance **quickly.** Into this moment of history steps God's answer to Israel's prayers.

Who did God bring to rule his people?

_____

Who was Deborah? She was the ultimate working mom. God's woman for the hour emerges on the scene with strength and calm determination. She has nerves of steel, lives a life submitted to the Holy Spirit, and is as wise as a world-class family therapist. (She also was a songwriter, but we'll talk about that later.)

Read Judges 4:4-5.

Where did Deborah live?

_____

To whom was she married?

_____

What was her job description?

_____

Where was her office?

_____

Deborah's law office was well-known. Her judgments were filled with wisdom.

In verse 5, who came to her and why?

_____

_____

Deborah has quite the resume, and these first two verses are astounding. Here is one of only five women in the Bible called a "prophetess." Here is **the only woman ever** called to serve as a judge in Israel.

In our modern world, it's hard for us to realize just how amazing this was in her culture. Today, we are not surprised to see women serving as judges. But Middle Eastern society has forever been patriarchal, and still is. Women were never seated in places of leadership and certainly had no authority over men. They were considered to be property. Their opinions were not sought out. Their job was to bear children, keep home, and keep quiet. (In other words, to stay barefoot and pregnant in the kitchen.)

Unlike the ego-driven men around Esther, Deborah lived in the hill country, surrounded by men refusing to take control. So this mother of Israel was used of God to "parent" his people. Deborah wisely directed people in how to live. She restored village life, meaning she re-wove the social structure. She was as good a judge in peacetime as in wartime." And when the hour came, she suited up in army gear and met her enemy on a literal battlefield with muddy men by her side. Where were her headquarters?

Read Judges 4:5 and let's take a look at her office.

What was the tree called?

_____

Her courtroom was held under the Palm of Deborah. This implies great respect. The association of her name with a palm tree tells us of the widespread regard for her judicial decisions.

"Deborah," according to the *NIV Study Bible*, "means 'bee.' [45] The Hebrew word for honey refers to both bee's honey and the sweet syrupy juice of dates. Deborah, the Bee, dispensed the sweetness of justice as she held court, not in a city gate where male judges sat, but under the shade of a 'honey' tree. Her style of leadership was gentle and loving. She had a way of judging that allowed the men in her society to trust her and not feel threatened.

Of all the twelve judges named in this book, none except Deborah is depicted as wise, talented, brilliant, and godly. Perhaps this is why she set up shop under a palm tree. Date palm trees hold special significance in biblical history.

Read Leviticus 23:40. What festival required the branches and fruit of palm trees?

_____

Turn to John 12:1. What feast was being observed?

_____

Now read John 12:13. What happened and what was used?

_____

_____

God's deliverance of the Hebrew nation from Egypt was celebrated each year during Passover. They would build booths with the branches of a palm tree and delight in its sweet, life-giving fruit. When Jesus rode into Jerusalem during Passover to become the sacrificial lamb for all people, the crowds waved beautiful palm tree branches before him shouting, "Blessed is he who comes in the name of the Lord!"

The palm design also was used as a decoration in the Temple of Solomon (1 Kings 6:29). As we bring Deborah's story to life, think of how she lived out this description of a date-palm from *Jewish Encyclopedia*:

"The stem of a date-palm is slender and very yielding, so that in a storm it sways back and forth, but does not break. The date-palm relies for nourishment upon its roots, which strike downward and reach water under the soil." [46]

Like the palm tree, Deborah drew strength from a deep-rooted trust in God. Downward she struck into the constancy of Jehovah's covenant. She arbitrated disputes between people. It was her wisdom they called upon to settle arguments and legal matters. On a daily basis, she would have listened to the arguments of angry citizens who wanted her to rule in their favor. She would have settled estates. Her solid grounding in the Lord sharpened her skill in listening to both sides of a matter and choosing the fairest choice of action. The depth of faith which gave her the ability to judge wisely also served her well when it was time for Israel to take to the battlefield. Rooted in Jehovah, she made each brave decision without losing her way. She faced the storm of war that came and inspired a nation to believe in God's power again. Without flinching she led an army into battle and never broke a spiritual sweat.

Deborah was called by many titles; she was a woman who wore many hats.

In Judges 5:7, how does she refer to herself?

_____

She was a powerful woman in a man's world. Yet even with all this authority, Deborah saw herself in a different light. Deborah arose as a mother in Israel. This was a title sparingly used in the Word. It was a title of honor, respect, and prominence. As Deborah viewed her role in God's plan, she saw herself first as a mother.

The great commentator Warren Wiersbe makes the point that "for God to give his people a female judge was to treat them like little children, which is exactly what they were when it came to spiritual things." He also makes the point that in that male-dominated society, it was an act of humiliation for the Jews to sit under a woman when all they wanted was male leadership.

Yet who better than a good mother to guide and teach a sinful, wayward, strong-willed, stiff-necked, disobedient nation? Sound familiar? Can you relate? For those of you who are mothers, does this description remind you of your children at times?

_____

_____

DEBORAH'S DYSFUNCTIONAL FAMILY

In her role as a mother of Israel, Deborah had a full plate contending with God's children. Let's look for a moment at the cycle of behavior they were caught in at the time of the Judges.

Turn to Judges 21:25.

How does this describe God's children?

_____

One might say his people were acting like unruly kids who could have used a serious spanking or a major "time out." Obviously in the minds of the Jews at this time, there was no absolute truth. Everyone did what they wanted to do, regardless of the laws of God. If it felt right, they did it, no matter how the choice lined up with the code of behavior God had given them.

A QUICK SIDEBAR: Does this sound familiar as you would describe the current spiritual condition in the United States of America? Why or why not?

_____

_____

This was not what God wanted for his children, then or now. He had been very specific and intentional with them and had made his will known for their lives. He wanted them to live lives of holy obedience and to possess the land! But Israel was caught in a cycle of sin. There are three repeated phrases throughout the book of Judges which clearly reveal their sad pattern of behavior.

Round and round they went on a merry-go-round of disobedience.

The sons of Israel did evil in the sight of the Lord.
The sons of Israel cried out to the Lord.
God heard their cries and raised up a deliverer.

Judges 2:18 is a concise picture of the entire book of Judges.

Read it and write the phrase at the end that describes our father's heart for his children.

_____

_____

We can picture our father looking at his children saying, "This is **not** what I had in mind for you!"

Read Joshua 1:2-9.

In **verse 3**, what did God give them?

_____

What did God promise in **verses 5 and 9**?

_____

What was God's formula for success in **verses 7 and 8**?

_____

_____

These verses are God's commissioning of Joshua and his ideal for the lifestyle he desired for his children as they entered the Promised Land. But in Deborah's day, the Israelites were sadly under- achieving and missing the mark, to say the least.

To paraphrase these verses, God seems to be saying, "Moses is dead. The wandering is over. Get up. I've given you the mantle of authority. I've handed you the baton. Now get going!"

THINK THIS THROUGH: In a very real sense, God commissions us in much the same way. We are to "possess the land" for his name's sake by living as a city set on a hill, a light piercing the darkness that surrounds us. We have been given the blood of Jesus and the Holy Spirit as our inheritance. Each of us has a promised land specifically made for us to inhabit.

How would you characterize your promised land?

_____

_____

How do you feel God encouraging you to take this "land" in his name and with his leading?

_____

_____

In Joshua's farewell address to the leaders of Israel, he commissions them as well. Read **Joshua 23:4-13**.

What was Joshua's warning in **verses 12-13**?

_____

When we look at the times of Deborah, we see the children of Israel had not heeded Joshua's warning and were now suffering the consequences of their disobedience. Surely the Israelites huddled around their fires at night and wondered, *Where is Yahweh? Why has he allowed all this trouble to befall us? Doesn't he love us anymore? Doesn't he care?* When we are too close to our own disobedience, it's nearly impossible to see the real problem. We leave God little room to move or bless us when we continually dismiss his will.

There is a curious passage that tells us why God left some of the enemies in the Promised Land. **Read Judges 2:20-Judges 3:4.**

From what we read in **3:4**, why did God leave some of the nations in the land?

_____

In **3:2**, what did he want the next generation of Israelites to learn?

_____

This is huge. In his infinite mercy and wisdom, our father knows what to allow in our lives for us to learn how to make war. In the 1960s, the popular mantra was, "Make love, not war." But according to God's plan for maturing us, there are times when he wants us to make war! But what does he want us to fight?

As a parent with unruly, disobedient children on his hands, what might God have hoped to inspire in them by a call to arms?

_____

_____

If they never learned how to resist their enemies, then they would be consumed by them. The children of Israel who had not previously experienced war needed to learn how to fight. If there was no enemy this would seem cruel. But we fight a continual battle against the enemy of God. Fighting for our faith includes prayer, fasting, listening to God, and at times, taking physical action.

My (Nan's) dad was a person who was desperate to learn how to make war. When he was a teen-ager, the Japanese attacked Pearl Harbor and the United States was plunged into World War II. Dad was determined to become a soldier and fight for his country, so he literally ran toward the conflict.

His mother was extremely overly protective. Out of a fear of losing him, she went behind my father's back and arranged with their family physician to have my dad classified as "4F." This meant he was physically unfit to serve and could not enlist. Dad was furious. He decided to run away from home. He hitchhiked from Richmond, Virginia, to West Palm Beach, Florida. He slept on a park bench until he found a job as a bell hop at The Breakers Hotel so that he could eat until he was officially in the military. Then he went straight to the army enlistment headquarters, lied about his age, and signed up to be a paratrooper. He chose this branch of service because he felt it was the most dangerous branch of the military.

When I asked Dad why he did this, he said, "I knew one day I would have children who would ask me what I was doing during World War II. I wanted to be able to tell them, 'I fought.'"

Dad had a clear view of who the enemy was, and Dad was desperate to be a part of the battle, no matter what it cost him.

Spiritually, there always is a war going on for a Christian who longs to walk in godliness. We're either battling our own sinful nature, or pushing against and trying to resist the culture of our day. Following Christ means signing up for battle. It just comes with the territory.

Judges tells us that the Israelites did not recognize the Canaanites as their enemy. Because their guard was down, they were assimilated into Canaanite society. They were intermarrying with idol worshipers and were serving pagan gods. But God, with a capital "G," in his fierce jealousy for those who are his own, couldn't let this behavior go unchecked.

Make a list of five things you think God would see as your enemy.

1.

2.

3.

4.

5.

Do you have a battle plan? A war is only won if there is a strategy to follow and if the solider is equipped and prepared at all times.

Turn to Ephesians 6:10-18 and read God's description of the best-possible battle gear.

How do these verses encourage your heart to stand strong, covered in his power as you face your enemies?

_____

_____

There is no doubt we have a captain of the host who stands ready to lead us. Have you enlisted in his army? Are you ready for boot camp? (We could go on and on with this analogy, but you get the point.)

In Deborah's time, as in our own, nations and situations are left "in the land" for testing. God wanted Israel to learn war. He wanted to find out if they would fight. Would they obey him or not?

Like Israel, we are tested. Throughout our lifetimes, we have large and small tests. Some can last a long time and we wonder if we'll ever survive them. Others are like a pop quiz. They happen suddenly. Someone cuts you off in traffic. Someone leaves their cart in the middle of the aisle in the grocery store. How do you respond? It's a quick test of how much we're allowing the Holy Spirit to control us that day.

Why does God test us? Write a few reasons he does this.

_____

_____

_____

Maybe he tests us because he loves to see our character development and wants us to mature. As a father, he is eager for his children to grow into strength and knowledge. He is eager for us to reign and rule with his son one day over kingdoms in the New Earth. He is in the process of training us to reign and delights to see us look more and more like his son, painful as it is for us at times.

Perhaps too, God's heart is filled with joy as he watches us discover that we can defeat the enemy. When we trust him enough, and love him enough to fight back against the darkness until we have a breakthrough, victory in him is sweet indeed.

Make the battle we are studying apply to your own life.

In our times of testing, we have Jesus as our deliverer. The Holy Spirit deposited into our soul calls us to rise up and face our battles with the battle cry, "Greater is he that is in me than he that is in this world!"

In this time of Israel's testing, God raised up a deliverer who once again foreshadowed the power of the coming messiah. In the voice of a mother in Israel, the people were galvanized into new faith. Deborah's responsibility was to rally the troops and call them into battle.

Turn to Judges 4:6-10.

Who did Deborah summon?

_____

What was her question?

_____

What did she ask him to do?

_____

What was God's battle plan and what was his promise to Barak?

_____

_____

In **verse 8**, the handsome and courageous general commissioned by Deborah and raised up by God to deliver his people stepped forward boldly to make what request?

_____

Bless his heart. He was scared. Israel had no ready army and very few weapons. They were vastly outnumbered. He had no idea this battle would become the stuff of Israelite lore.

83:9-10 to see what was said of this victory after he was gone.

Editorial Comment: Women, we have the power to make or break the spirit of men. We can inspire or defeat a man with our words. In times of crisis, or when the men in our lives are down, feeling inadequate, or even fearful, how we respond can literally change the course of history. How we cringe when we hear a wife tear her husband down in public, or hear derogatory comments about how a son, cousin, brother, or even a student will "never amount to anything?" Let's remember that our words matter greatly to the men around us.

Read **Proverbs 31: 26**. How does a woman like Deborah speak?

_____

_____

Deborah inspired the men of Israel to rise up and fight for their nation. She spoke strength into despairing hearts and turned their faces to see God's unchanging gaze upon them. She knew how a man responded to R-E-S-P-E-C-T. Barak's request that she go into battle with him came from his awareness that she would build up the men. This woman lit a fire not by using derision or threats. She believed in the power of God to make the men of Israel strong again. Barak knew her presence would rally the men, inspire them and give them courage. Deborah had a way about her that wasn't threatening, that encouraged and did not belittle them. She was an inspirational leader; otherwise Barak would not have asked her to go with him.

NOTE TO SELF: In your own sphere of influence, how do you relate to those around you?

There are people who need you and look up to you. Believe it. If you're operating in grace, you're a magnet for those who are struggling for encouragement. No matter how old you are, and especially if you are over sixty , there are generations behind you that are watching. The sight of a mature woman still walking with Jesus after many years is a gift to all fortunate enough to see her.

Now turn to Hebrews 11:32-34.

Who is listed as a hero?

_____

In **verse 34**, what did the heroes accomplish?

_____

The defeat of Barak's enemies would one day become a legend among the Hebrews of how God's power and might were unleashed on behalf of his children. Barak never dreamed he'd be listed as a hero in the Hall of Faith when the writer of Hebrews penned his famous chapter. He didn't see himself in the light of eternity. He had a small picture of Yahweh and saw himself as a guy facing impossible odds.

Why list Barak and not Deborah?

This might seem strange at first. Didn't Deborah ask Barak to round up the guys for war? Didn't Deborah pose the question, *"Has not the Lord gone ahead of you?"* (NIV)

Compare Barak's request to Deborah in **verse 8** with a similar one in **Exodus 33:14-15**. Note the connection:

_____

_____

In Judges 4:9, who did Deborah say would receive the glory from the battle?

_____

Deborah's gift as a prophetess tells us the Holy Spirit had fallen specifically on her. Her statement about the glory of victory being given to woman was evidence of these prophetic gifts. She wasn't talking about herself. As we study the entire story we find that the battle Deborah led was finished by another woman named Jael. Two unlikely heroines arose from the army of Israel. Two brave-hearted women assisted Barak and his men. These two women confounded the wise, and literally put the fear of God into the enemy that day.

Barak represented the opinion everyone had of Deborah. All the men in her sphere of influence would have been aware that the presence of God was with her. When Moses requested the Lord's presence go with him as he led the people, so Barak's request mirrors this same faith in the power of God's Spirit.

Barak knew he would not receive glory from the battle. He didn't care that a woman would lead, because he knew Deborah's words spoke life. He showed great faith in asking for her presence as commander of the army.

As for Deborah, she showed tremendous humility and strategic wisdom in choosing to assemble a strong team to fight the battle. Her words encouraged those around her to remember the delivering power of Jehovah. With graceful integrity she then allowed the men and women in the battle to walk out their specific places of faith. Generous with the victory, Deborah credits God above all. As a spiritual, physical and mental leader she never oversteps her place with the men under her charge. She graciously allows the army of Israel to see themselves as victors, as honorable men, as God's chosen people. Scotty Smith wrote the following observation in his study on Judges:

*"Deborah cannot physically lead the army. Therefore she has to recruit someone who compl*ements her gifts. She is the only judge who does not accomplish the deliverance single-handedly. There are not one, but three "channels" by which God destroys the oppressors: Deborah, Barak, and Jael. While male judges are highly independent and warlike, Deborah is a team builder who creates interdependence between leaders. She identifies, recruits, and encourages. She is a team builder, not the lone ranger." [47]

This brave judge/mother/wife/songwriter/motivational speaker/prophetess now dons military gear and then becomes commander of Israel's army. Deborah balances her many gifts with a pervasive sense of humility and trust in God. She knows the people who have visited her under the Palm. She knows the history of God's covenant and faithfulness. She also is aware of the abysmal history of failure in Israel to do what was right in the sight of the Lord.

Yet Deborah sees beyond the circumstances of her day and believes God is greater than Israel's sin. It's time, her time, to lead them into battle against the enemy. With God going before them, Deborah is focused on a miraculous victory.

ISRAEL FIGHTS A NEW GOLIATH

DID THE JUDGE HAVE HER OWN TENT OR BUNK WITH THE BOYS?

Verse 9 ends with the phrase, "And Deborah arose!" (Amplified Bible).

She stood up. She laced up her hiking boots and hoisted her skirts. She camped out with the guys and marched shoulder-to-shoulder with the troops. Wow. What a woman.

Put your name in the middle of this phrase: "And _____ arose!"

By any worldly calculation, Deborah and the army of Israel were in for a massive defeat. In taking to the battlefield against the imposing army led by Sisera, Israel would surely be slaughtered. This period in history was the close of the Bronze Age and the Iron Age was beginning. Nations with the technological skill to develop iron tools and chariots were virtually undefeatable against lesser armies. These chariots were swift, maneuverable weapons. An iron chariot could cut through men on the ground "like a hot knife through butter." [48]

According to Judges 4:13, how many chariots did Sisera command?

_____

For the scorekeepers, that would be 900 chariots more than Israel had. Nine hundred to zero. The chariots easily would have taken the day. But verse 13 also lets us know that Sisera had many men with him as well. Sisera had the latest advanced weaponry and home-field advantage.

Read Judges 4:10-16.

How many men made up the army of Israel?

_____

Our Lord delights in doing the impossible. As C. S. Lewis said, "To God, crisis is an atmosphere for miracles." As we study this through, we are invited to keep our own personal battles in mind. With every detail of the victory, remember you and I serve the same God who gave Sisera into the hands of the "weaker" sex and a vastly overwhelmed army.

Read Judges 4:14.

Deborah gave Barak a huge gift before he plunged into battle. What did she say to him in this verse?

_____

"Up!"

This was Deborah's pep talk to Barak and the soldiers before they went out to face their enemies. *"The Lord has gone out before you!" We don't know if Deborah got this information in the moment as a prophetic word from God or if she was remembering another time in Israel's history.*

Read Deuteronomy 9:1-3.

What did Moses tell the Israelites God was doing for them?

_____

Why was Deborah so confident of the final outcome? She knew her God. She saw beyond her circumstances. Again we hear her encouraging, cheerleading, unafraid, and leading the charge. She knows they are outnumbered and that in human eyes there is no way they can win. She looks out at them quaking in their boots and says, "OK guys, this is your defining moment. It is the day you will refer to for the rest of your lives as the time you were the most alive. For generations to come, your children will speak of what God has done for you today. Go forth mightily in the strength of the one true God! Once more into the breach, my friends, once more!"

PERSONAL FUN TIME-OUT: Write a pep talk for your best friend. How would you encourage her? Look at her circumstances through the eyes of eternity. Remember that the Lord has gone before her to give her victory in whatever she is facing. Write it down and speak it over her or send it to her in the mail. Help send her back into her battles with renewed courage and strength.

_____

_____

Now let's find out exactly what happened in Deborah's battle. **Read Judges 4:15-16.**

What happens to the army of Sisera?

_____

_____

All those chariots and not a one survived. During the battle, God caused a torrential rainstorm to beat down into the battlefield. Then the Kishon River overflowed. It made a muddy mess that made it impossible for Sisera to use those high-tech chariots. God also caused a spirit of confusion and panic to seize the enemy soldiers. At this point, all the Israelites had to do was finish them off. All those men, and every last one fell by the sword. Well, almost every last one. The one who got away met his end by the hands of another woman used of God.

Who ran from the battlefield?

_____

Sisera reminds us of satan. As soon as we use the weapons of our warfare (2 Corinthians 10:3-4) in battle against him, he has to flee. Brave and arrogant Sisera, the commander of 900 chariots and countless warriors, is fleeing on foot! He's a coward. He doesn't have the courage to fight and die alongside his men. He runs away, and into the dangerous hospitality of a bold and godly woman.

Turn to Judges 4:17-24 to learn the fate of Sisera.

Who lands the final blow to the enemy?

_____

Read it and don't weep. The courage of Deborah was contagious! Another woman was inspired to arise. Jael knew what to do to her enemies. She saw Sisera coming and went out to meet him. By this time, he was the last soldier standing. But Jael wanted to make sure her enemy was completely routed. She could not let him get away, but the job wasn't finished.

A TIME FOR WAR!

THE WHOLE PICTURE: Two women were the undoing of Sisera. Commentaries on the story help put this gory story into perspective. They note that Sisera's men had tormented the women of Israel for two decades.

Turn for a moment and **read Judges 5:28-30.**

Who was looking for Sisera out the window?

_____

When the sound of his chariot's horses did not arrive, what explanation was given?

It was common practice for enemies like Sisera to steal, rape, and torment women as spoils of war. His mom was muttering under her breath, wondering with the women around her about how long it was taking for Sisera and his army to divvy up their spoils. Many men took two women for each man and did with them whatever they liked. In Hebrew, the word "girl" would have been more accurately translated "wench" or "girl-slave." The women captured in the "spoils" would be sex slaves to their enemies.

In God's hands of justice, we are left to marvel that two women were used by God to take the life of Sisera. Two women bringing down one evil man. Sounds about right.

Another interesting note: Women in ancient Israel were responsible for setting up and taking down the family tent. The use of hammers and tent pegs would have been a part of everyday life. Jael had most likely been abused and witnessed the rape and nightmare treatment of her girlfriends at his hands. She would have handled a hammer and pin as easily as a kitchen rolling pin. Murder and lying do not line up with God's commandments on healthy living. Yet it's not difficult to understand why Jael had no problem driving one of her tent pegs into the unsuspecting head of Sisera.

GOT MILK?

As for Jabin the king, read **Judges 4: 23-24** and describe how he met his maker:

God subdued the king, and the Israelies bore down on him until he was utterly destroyed. Once again, the God of many chances delivers his people.

How do we drive a tent peg into the head of our enemy? First, we must know that the battle is the Lord's. We must believe he has gone before us to give us the victory. We must fight until the job is done.

Deborah is ready to celebrate with her people. It's time to kick off the party! The victory is so glorious Deborah had to write a song about it. The spontaneous worship that flowed from her soul proclaimed the Lord, the God of Israel, as the one worthy of all her praise.

In Judges 5 read Deborah's victory song.

In **Judges 5:1** who sang with her?

This is one of the most poetic, beautiful tributes to God in the entire Bible. As you read the chapter, it's as if one can hear the duet passed between Deborah and Barak, sharing the joy and praise.

In **verse 2 and verse 9** they tell and retell one phrase.

What was Deborah so happy about?

_____

Who do they honor?

_____

What was the heart attitude honored?

_____

Leaders and commanders in Israel willingly offered themselves for battle. It was no little thing to follow a female commander into a fight against an enemy with 900 iron chariots. These leaders led with hearts of faith that God would move on their behalf. Or perhaps they offered themselves willingly to honor their nation and families, no matter the outcome.

What is said at the end of each of these verses?

_____

Godly leaders make us all want to shout, "Bless the Lord!" Finally someone stood up and led the way. Finally there are voices that say, "No" to the enemy of God. Finally we can see revival and hope come alive again in the faces of those who seek after God's heart.

What kind of person makes you say, "Bless the Lord?"

_____

_____

What must happen for leaders to be respected?

_____

Risk. True leaders risk even their lives for the cause of doing the right thing. And when they risk, it's like a holy virus that spreads through the people around them. Risking our lives in the hands and providence of God is a sure choice.

What happens to godly leaders? People follow. They have someone to set the example, and like Deborah and Barak, new leaders light fires of new hope and faith.

In **verse 7**, what was the turning point that changed the course of the story?

_____

Read Judges 5:10-11. In Deborah's song what did she ask the people of Israel to do?

_____

"Rehearse the righteous acts of the Lord, even the righteous acts toward his villagers in Israel" (Amplified Bible). Rehearse, remember, recall, review the power of God. Tell it to your children, your neighbors, your coworkers. Tell it to yourself! Remember the Lord is faithful. Rehearse and repeat until it's part of your daily habits.

In Judges 5, the song of Deborah is a shared moment of celebration between herself, Barak, and a newly restored nation of Israel. Like little children on Christmas morning, they delight over every gift of the victory.

The opening verses sing, in essence, *"Remember how bad off we* were, how tired and beaten down. Then you came, Deborah, rising up, a mother of Israel. Yes, we will rehearse this over and over and oh, yes! Did we mention how grateful we are for leaders who are willing to put themselves on the line?"

In **verses 13-18** who does Deborah list?

_____

_____

She goes through each tribe of Israel to honor the nobles and leaders that showed up when called by Barak. Strong words of praise are used for the tribes who shared in the battle. Out of the twelve, Deborah ticks off the names of the five and a half who participated. Then in front of God and everyone she lists the ones who were a no-show. It's as if Deborah is saying:

"How could you dare to miss the excitement of this moment? You missed all the fun in watching what God did for our people. Tribe of Reuben, was it really more interesting to listen to bleating sheep on the hills? Gilead, you guys just hung back in Jordan. Dan, why did you stay with the ships? Asher, you were sunbathing on the seacoasts and fishing in your creeks. We will sing of the victory, but you all missed out!"

Next they sing a vigorous chorus about the battle itself.

In **verses 4, 21-22** we find the details of how God gave the Israelites power over the chariots. Describe what happened.

_____

_____

_____

Can you say, "flash-flood warning?" Let us never forget who holds the universe and everything under the sun.

Turn and read Luke 8:24-25.

Describe how Jesus spoke to the weather conditions that day.

_____

_____

_____

This is one of my favorite passages in scripture. Jesus *"censured, blamed, and rebuked the wind and the raging waves"* (Amplified Bible). In effect, the one who made all things said to his creation, 'Calm down, be still, and hush up!'

In **Judges 5:20** what other element of creation assisted the Israelites?

Yes, from the heavens the stars in their courses joined in and fought against Sisera. This was a true *Star Wars* spectacular!

The closing of Deborah's song sings of the brave and bloody death of Sisera at the hands of Jael. Keep in mind how many women had been disgraced by Jabin's army, and how desperate their situation. The women of God had been used as sex slaves, humiliated and shamed before their men and children.

We find it utterly liberating as women to read of Deborah's bold proclamations. God allowed women to take the day, to inspire their men, to free Israel from bondage and to live again with dignity and honor.

Look at verse 31. Deborah ends her song with yet another word of encouragement. Isn't this beautiful? She gives one final picture of what we all are like when we love and follow Jesus. We are like the rising of the sun in its might.

One mother stood up. A mother named Deborah. And when she did, a nation was transformed.

We have studied the lives of two women who demonstrated the power of equality without picket lines or demanding rights. Deborah and Esther embraced the God-given characteristics of being a woman and used each one to its full capacity.

They inspire us today with their ability to maximize every ounce of their womanhood in serving God's purposes. Neither woman was ashamed to fight the enemy as God's lady. Both retained their femininity while standing strong and staring down evil. Like Esther, Deborah shines as a role model for all women who love the Lord. Both women remind us of our identity in God. The true liberation and rights of his women are defined by God alone.

Like Deborah, like Esther, when we obey his call, face down in prayer, we can rise up and defeat our enemies. Jesus put to rest any question about how God feels about his women. We are made in his image by his hands and given tools to pin down the enemy with the blood of a risen savior. When we face our battlefield, we can move ahead with victory in our father God and enjoy being his girl.

Our best days are ahead. While our outer bodies are decaying, we are like the rising of the sun, growing brighter and stronger and fierce toward our enemy. We were meant to make the demons tremble. Do you feel heroic? Probably not. When you're knee-deep in the mud of battle, it's hard to feel like singing a victory song. But heroes are made one gritty, dirty foxhole at a time, and when we follow God, we rout the enemy. The battles we face today are the stuff of heaven's lore. *"O my soul, march on with strength!"*

Let's follow Deborah's lead and sign up for the army of God. As we arrive for a pep talk under her Palm Tree we just might read this sign hanging on her office wall:

"Women of the Living God: BE ALL THAT YOU CAN BE!"

Epilogue

Mega congratulations to you beloved friend!

We thank you for taking a journey with us through the lives of our heroines of faith. You stepped off into the deep end of the pool, immersing yourself in this study using the Sword of God's Word and your sanctified imagination. Both should be sharper for the wear.

These women from Biblical history who dared to believe God have thrown down the gauntlet to all of us. They chose to trust in the character of God during times of doubt, despair, famine, widowhood, barren seasons, war and even great national apostasy. Their lives were a wild ride of faith, proving once and for all that following God's lead is always an adventure.

Our prayer is that you feel you know these women as flesh and blood sisters of the faith. They were women like you and me, filled with hormones and dreams and longings to find purpose in God. By walking for a few weeks in their shoes, we see that not much has changed through the centuries. The fallen garden affects all our lives with a need to look for meaning behind the seen. Eventually we are left to decide what we will do with the covenant promises of God that lead to the scarlet cross of Jesus.

These women we have studied didn't have the bigger picture we enjoy. But the blood of Christ runs both ways – before and after the hill on Calvary. These women who lived before us knew that Yahweh was the covenantal God of the Ages. They insistently believed He would come through with His promise of the Messiah. They were willing to do anything to be a part of His story.

As we investigated the lives and times of these women, we could just as easily be reading a page from the journals of our own century. The dust of time still kicks up a raging storm in the here and now of our lives.

Will we reach out like our fore sisters and lay claim to our place in the lineage of Christ?

Will we dare to believe He is all we need?

Let's do this thing! Let's dare to be His girls in a world desperate to see authentic women seeking His heart.

We are honored to join you as we walk on, strengthened by our mutual faith. With the grace of Jesus, empowered by the Holy Spirit may we show others what it looks like to be mothers, sisters and daughters of the living God.

Most humbly in Him,
Nan and Bonnie

Leader's Guide and Study Questions

We all know it's one thing to read the Bible or do a study on your own, but quite another to share it with your best girlfriends. Because we've *learned so much about God, ourselves, and each other through our* three-decade, hand-in-hand walk, we wanted to give you the same opportunity. After you complete each week's session, be sure to gather with other women who dare to believe. We promise it will be worth your while.

These gatherings can be informal, but it might help to designate a facilitator, just to make sure the conversation keeps on track. It's also OK to switch up the facilitator each week. Regardless, a few things to keep in mind:

Start each meeting in prayer, fully expecting God to move. Follow with a brief recap of the previous week's *lesson in case someone was unable to keep up* or attend.

Allow the Spirit to lead. Realize that some of these lessons may necessitate times of personal confession, ministry, or prayer. Find a balance between staying on track and taking care of business!

Consider setting an ending time for your gatherings. Formally dismiss at that time, but note that people can still stay around and chat further (as long as it's OK with the hostess).

Encourage some sort of communication during the week. It doesn't have to be official prayer partners, but do find a way to touch base.

Draw out those who aren't participating by creating a safe, respectful atmosphere. Be sure, though, that nobody feels put on the spot.

Don't feel like you have to get through all of the questions during a meeting. We've included a lot here, knowing that some will work better for your group than others. These are just jumping off points. Sometimes a discussion will lead to unexpected revelation. Go with it.

Remember to have fun!

WEEK ONE DISCUSSION QUESTIONS: The Midwives of Egypt

What was the political climate when Moses was born?

How do the political circumstances during the time of Moses' birth mirror ours today?

We are daily called upon to push against the culture of our times and live differently. What forces push against us? According to Scripture, how do we push back?

The Egyptians were cruel to the Israelites because they were afraid of them. The Egyptians saw potential and were threatened. When satan looks at believers, he sees a threat to him and his kingdom. How are believers a threat to satan and his agenda? How does he attempt to harass us? How can we respond?

Which biblical Vitamin "C" for Courage verse did you choose to memorize? Why?

Share something God has called you to midwife.

What women have encouraged and nurtured you in your faith?

What risks are you willing to take in order to faithfully walk on the path of obedience to God?

It is not politically correct today to openly proclaim that you are a Christian. What does this require of us? What issues in our current political climate most need the influence of Christians?

The story of the courage of the midwives was told and retold to future generations of Israelites. What decisions are you making today that could affect generations to come?

Pray for each other to be strong in the days ahead. Ask God to give your best friend and

you the courage you need to safely deliver what he has entrusted to you.

WEEK TWO DISCUSSION QUESTIONS: Jochebed

How do you think Jochebed hid Moses for 3 months?

Why did she launch him into the Nile?

What stories from the past would the Hebrews have been recalling in order to gain strength for the hard times they were facing?

Jochebed believed she had something to hope for, in spite of the law of the land. In what do we place our hope?

What are the greatest threats to children in our culture? How do we protect them?

Jochebed took her most treasured possession and let it go. She launched Moses directly

into her enemy's hands. What treasures of your heart have you had to let go? What sustains you in this act of faith?

How could Jochebed bear knowing that her son was being raised by idol worshippers? We send our kids out into the world today to face ungodly teachers, friends, movies, TV, employers, etc. How do we prepare them?

We would not choose an idol worshiper to have great influence over the lives of people we love. What unlikely people has God used in your life to accomplish his purposes?

How was God sovereign in this story? Looking back, how have you seen the hand of God guiding your life?

Spend some time in prayer for one another, asking God to keep you faithful as he sovereign-

ly unfolds his plans for your family.

Jochebed may have wondered, Where is God in my circumstances? Has he forgotten me?" Jochebed did not know Moses was the deliverer of the Hebrew nation. She just did the next right thing she knew to do. We don't know the final results of our obedience either. How does Jochebed's story encourage you?

WEEK THREE DISCUSSION QUESTIONS: Miriam

What do you think it was like for Miriam, a teen-age girl growing up in a Hebrew ghetto in a police state? Much of her life was "underground." What kind of personalities can this life-style create? Was hers a life of fear or faith?

How do you think she felt about standing in crocodile-infested waters, hiding in bulrushes? What risks was she taking while standing guard over baby Moses?

Why was Miriam's approach of the princess risky? What were the potential dangers?

Discuss the quote by Corrie ten Boom, "Faith is like radar that sees through the fog—the reality of things at a distance that the human eye cannot see." Are you straining to see something through the fog, believing there is something on the other side? Is there someone you're watching from spiritual bulrushes, praying for their deliverance?

What do you imagine Miriam was doing those forty years while Moses was living in the palace?

When Moses led the Israelites out of Egypt, he was eighty. Miriam was in her mid-nineties. Read Exodus 15:20-21. Discuss what this moment meant to Miriam.

When the Israelites leave Egypt and go to the wilderness, Moses, Aaron, and Miriam share a leadership role. Read Numbers 12:1-15. What happened? Can anyone identify with feeling overlooked or underappreciated?

Do you think Miriam finished well? Read Micah 6:4 and Exodus 15:20-21. What was Miriam called?

Our faith, not our works, is accounted to us as righteousness. Read and discuss Malachi

3:14-18. Discuss God's choice of record-keeping in heaven. How does this make you feel? There is no record kept of a believer's sins. Are you keeping a record of someone else's sins?

As one who fears the Lord and esteems his name, begin keeping a "Book of Remembrance" and record specific answers to your prayers while taking this study. Share it with a trusted friend.

WEEK FOUR DISCUSSION QUESTIONS: The Princess of Egypt

Why do you think the princess defied her father's law and took a Hebrew baby into the palace, raising him as her own son? What does this tell us about her personality?

Read Proverbs 21:1 and Daniel 2:21. What do these verses tell us about all who hold political power?

Why do you think God uses people who do not call him Lord to accomplish his purposes?

Read Acts 7:21-22. How would you describe Moses' education in the palace? What kind of expectations do you think the princess had for Moses? What do you think her reaction was when Moses left after killing the Egyptian?

The midwives, Jochebed, Miriam, and the princess all had to let go of something and accept the consequences. What did it cost them? What did they gain? How do their choices apply to us today?

None of these women knew they were playing out a very specific role in God's plan for the ages. Each one of them was taking life one day at a time and doing what they thought was right. In light of this truth, how should we view our daily obedience to God's calling on our life?

Moses' life began at a time in Egypt when Hebrew sons were being killed. After the death angel came to Egypt and Moses led the sons of Israel out to the Promised Land, the Egyptians knew what it felt like to lose their sons. Discuss the justice of God and the principle of sowing and reaping.

Do you identify with any of the women we have studied so far? Why?

WEEK FIVE DISCUSSION QUESTIONS: Rahab

Read Isaiah 45:4-5. According to this verse, who does the choosing when it comes to salvation?

Read John 6:37, 44, 45. How do we come to God? Who does the calling? Who does the saving?

Read Ephesians 1:4. When were we chosen? In whom are we found?

What had Rahab heard about the deeds of Yahweh?

How did she respond? How did the rest of Jericho respond? Compare this to the response of Jezebel when fire from heaven came down and God clearly consumed the altar of sacrifice. Even in the face of overwhelming evidence, some simply refuse to believe.

What mighty work did Rahab do that gave her a place in the lineage of Jesus? She simply believed. What makes us righteous before God? Discuss Romans 4:3.

Are you trusting in works to make you righteous before God? Why do we sometimes not want to believe it is by faith alone that we are saved?

Rahab's world literally crumbled around her when the walls of Jericho fell. What do you think it was like for her as she listened to her city be destroyed? Do you think she wondered if the spies would keep their promise to save her? Do you feel at times your world is collapsing around you? What promises can you cling to?

How do you think the Hebrew women responded when they heard the spies had hidden in the house of a prostitute? Or when Rahab joined the Israelite camp? Why is it hard for us to accept some of the people God chooses?

Discuss labels we give each other. Do you feel labeled? Why?

Read Matthew 21:28-32. Who was Jesus most angry with in this story?

Discuss reasons why non-religious people like Rahab may be quicker to accept salvation and believe God than those who may feel good about their life choices.

Why do you think Rahab was attracted to the story of a slave nation being delivered from bondage? How does her story parallel that of the Israelites?

How was Rahab like the midwives in Egypt?

Why do you think the spies went to a prostitute's house?

What does the scarlet cord symbolize for us? What did it symbolize for the Israelites?

Is there anyone you consider past the hope of redemption? Does God?

Choose some adjectives to describe Rahab. What adjectives does Jesus use to describe you?

The eyes of the Lord roam the earth looking for those whose hearts are turned toward him. How does this encourage you?

WEEK SIX DISCUSSION QUESTIONS: Tamar

Did Tamar see herself as a victim?

What power did she have in choosing the course of her life?

How did Judah view Tamar?

Why do you think Tamar fought so hard to have an heir and a place in Judah's family line? What did she see in this family that was worth holding on to?

How did Judah's behavior toward Tamar contrast with God's plan for the care of widows?

In Genesis 38:26, why do you think Judah called Tamar "righteous?"

Read Matthew 1:3. Who is Jesus descended from? No situation is too messy for God. Tamar literally wrestled with God in her own way and he blessed her with a place in the lineage of Jesus. Does anything about God's choice of Tamar make you uncomfortable?

Read Jeremiah 1:5 and 29:11. Discuss God's big picture for your life.

The story of Judah and Tamar shows us that God uses even our failures to accomplish

his purposes. How does this apply to your life and bring comfort? How has God brought beauty from your ashes?

Read Ruth 4:12. What Jewish blessing was pronounced over Ruth and Boaz?

Tamar is a study in desperation. How do we find connection to Tamar? None of us have to sleep our way into the family of God. We don't earn our salvation, but to what lengths are you willing to go to fulfill your destiny in Jesus? What do you desire desperately?

Tamar wanted safety and security. Where is our security found?

WEEK SEVEN DISCUSSION QUESTIONS: Tamar, daughter of David

Tamar probably spent her lifetime trying to recover from rape. What words of comfort and hope would Jesus give Tamar?

What happens when we keep secret those things in our lives that should be brought to light? Read Psalm 51:6 and discuss the application of this verse to our hidden past experiences.

What does God say about our behavior toward the weak? How seriously does he take it when someone is abused?

What was the Old Testament punishment for rape?

When will we see the complete justice of God? To whom is the execution of his justice directed?

What does the enemy of our souls try to say to us regarding sexual abuse in our past? Are there condemning tapes playing over and over in your head, full of lies from satan? How do we counteract them with truth?

Why do you think there is so much sexual assault against women and children today? What message is our culture sending to men about women? What messages are women sending to men?

Amnon pretended to be ill and afraid of being poisoned. After all, he was the firstborn son of the King and next in line for the throne, so naturally he'd be a target for assassination. But why did everyone have to leave the room before he ate Tamar's cooking? What was she thinking? What warning does this give the modern woman about where we go and whose company we keep?

What choices in David's history bore fruit in the behavior of Amnon?

Tamar had a healthy reaction to her pain. Why do you think the men in her life covered it up? Why were they not willing to face it?

If David had disciplined Amnon, how could that have changed the future events that unraveled after Tamar's rape?

When Amnon committed sexual immorality and Absolom committed murder, they became guilty of the sins of their father David. When we choose to walk in sin, there are consequences that affect not only us but those around us. What hope does God offer for the breaking of the cycle of sin in our lives?

Look at Psalm 51. This was written after David sinned with Bathsheba. How was David different from Amnon?

As the firstborn son of the king, Amnon had a sense of entitlement. How does this attitude destroy character? Have you ever felt "above the law?"

Discuss the ways we grieve today. Are we socially "allowed" to fully express our grief?

All abused women are looking for rescue, waiting for the hero to ride up, destroy her abuser, and take her away to a place of safety where she will be cherished and protected. Is there any human being who can do this for us? Will there be justice done on our behalf? Who can do this? Who wants to do this for us? Read Isaiah 57:15 and discuss God's role in our lives as healer.

WEEK EIGHT DISCUSSION QUESTIONS: Leah

In Genesis, the glorious book of beginnings, we read the story of the God of the universe creating the world, the fall of mankind, the flood of Noah, and the creating of all nations. Then we follow the patriarchs: Abraham, Isaac, Jacob and Joseph. In this sweeping book that covers a span of 2300 years, we find the story of Leah, an unattractive and unloved woman. Why would the Holy Spirit guide Moses to tell her story? And in such detail? Out of all the important events that happen in Genesis, why did Moses give five chapters to the story of this woman? Is it by accident that God included this story in the book that is the foundation piece of the history of mankind?

The house of Laban takes the term "dysfunctional family" to new heights. What does this

tell us about the kinds of people God uses to accomplish his purposes? What encouragement can we find in this truth?

What similarities do you see between Jacob's treatment of Isaac and Laban's treatment of Jacob? Discuss the application of the phrase "what goes around comes around" in the regard to what happened on Jacob's wedding night.

Both Jacob and Laban were masters of deceit and manipulation. What fruit did it bear in their lives?

How was Jacob a "work in progress?"

Leah was raised on the story of how Abraham's servant met her Aunt Rebekah by divine appointment at a well and showered her with gifts and took her away to be the chosen bride of Isaac. How do you think this romantic story affected Leah and her own personal dreams as she was growing up?

What messages in our culture today set women up for disappointment?

What did Leah want? How did she go about trying to get it?

What do you think those seven years were like for Leah as she watched Rachel anticipate her wedding?

What is it like to be obsessed with obtaining something you can't have? Where would God have us focused instead? What hope does God offer us in place of our obsessions?

Leah had a nickname that doesn't sound very complimentary. How do you think it affected her self-image? What power does a name have over us? What does self-doubt do to us if allowed to dominate our lives?

What would Jesus say to the woman who feels she does not "measure up?"

What is the fruit of competition between women as it applies to beauty, clothing, or status?

How did Laban view his daughters? How did this affect Leah's view of herself?

Why didn't Laban arrange for a husband for Leah during those first seven years? What do you think he was planning all along and why?

Do you think Leah was a willing or reluctant participant in the scheme to deceive Jacob?

Why?

Why do you think Jacob didn't know it was Leah in the wedding tent?

What do you think the morning after was like for Leah? What behavior did this set in motion for her for the rest of her life?

What was Leah and Rachel's relationship like for the rest of their lives?

After Jacob "fulfilled Leah's week" how would you describe their marriage?

What did Leah hope would happen each time she bore Jacob a son?

Leah found her self-worth in her children. What does God want our self-worth to be anchored in?

As the bride of Christ, how does Jesus see us? In light of this, how should we see ourselves?

Someone once said, "Faith is living without scheming." How could this apply to our story of

Jacob and Leah and Rachel? How does it apply to us?

From the names she gave her sons, what can we conclude about Leah's relationship with Yahweh?

Leah went from a lifetime of self-doubt, disappointment, and unfulfilled dreams to a place in the crimson line: the lineage of Jesus Christ. What do you think Leah would say to us, her sisters, today?

WEEK NINE DISCUSSION QUESTIONS: Rachel

The role of the father in the development of a daughter is crucial to her sense of self-worth. Discuss Laban's style of parenting his daughters. How did if affect Rachel's concept of her value as a woman?

No dads are perfect. Human fathers will fail us. If we didn't get the affirmation of our femininity from our dads that we needed, where do we go for help and healing? Where should we not go?

What does it mean to wait for someone to "fill up your dance card?"

You can have a house full of children and still be barren. What does it mean to have "barrenness of the soul?"

Laban, Caleb, Saul, and Lot were willing to give their daughters in exchange for something they wanted. How did Jesus change forever the status of women?

Discuss the term "reversal of fortune," How does it apply to this story? To ours?

What is the meaning of the phrase, "God is never finished?" How does it apply to the characters in the story of Leah and Rachel?

Read Philippians 2:14. How would this verse have comforted Leah and Rachel? How does

it comfort you?

Read Zephaniah 3:14-17. Does this verse change the way you think of yourself? How? In light of the truth contained in this verse, what would Rachel say to us today?

Imagine a conversation between Leah and Rachel while Rachel is on her death bed. What words of reconciliation could have occurred?

Leah raised Joseph and Benjamin after Rachel's death. How do you imagine this could have been healing for Leah as she held Benjamin on her lap and said, "Let me tell you about your mother?"

Read Psalm 139:13. The weaver's loom is used to describe the process of our creation in the womb. How does God see you? How can this change the way you see yourself?

Discuss the quote from Eleanor Roosevelt, "No one can make you feel inferior without your consent."

WEEK TEN DISCUSSION QUESTIONS: Esther, part one

What do you think it was like for the people of Persia to be ruled by a king like Xerxes? How secure could they feel in his leadership? How does this story motivate you to pray for our current world leaders?

What kind of people did Xerxes surround himself with? Discuss the phrase, "We are known by the company we keep."

Discuss Mordecai and Esther's relationship. What foundational truths can we assume Esther learned from Mordecai about their shared heritage?

Why do you think some Jews stayed in Persia when they could have gone home to Israel?

How do we live in a godless place and remain godly? Do you ever feel displaced? Out of step spiritually with your surroundings?

What do you think of Vashti's choice to not be paraded at Xerxes' party? How did her choice affect all the women in the kingdom?

Based on Esther 2:8-15, how would you describe Esther?

What do you think it cost Esther to be chosen by Xerxes? What did she give up by being chosen as his queen? What losses did she have to grieve in her life?

Put yourself in Esther's sandals. You've been raised by someone other than your biological mother or father. You are living in a culture where you are a minority. Your faith and customs are considered odd by the people who do not share your religious heritage. You have hopes and dreams for a certain path you want your life will take. Then suddenly, against your will, your life takes a completely unexpected turn. You have to put aside your dreams and follow a road you didn't choose. How do you react? How do we handle our disappointment with the way some things turn out in our lives?

Why do you think a man like Xerxes was attracted to a woman like Esther?

Discuss the statement, "Esther's circumstances changed but they didn't change her." What kept Esther grounded in the truth of who she was? What must we be grounded in if we're to go forward without all the answers?

Moses, Jonah, and Jesus all asked God for another way to do his will. When we hit a crossroads and feel inadequate for the task, what do we do?

WEEK ELEVEN DISCUSSION QUESTIONS: Esther, part two

Mordecai laid some pretty heavy words on Esther when he told her she had "come to the kingdom for such a time as this." Go to Acts 17:26. What does this say about the time and place you were born? How do you feel the events of your life—and how you are living it—are having an impact on those around you? What does it mean to understand your hour?

Do you feel your place in this world happened randomly? Do you believe God has brought you to this moment "for such a time as this?" What evidence do you see?

Read John 15:16 and Ephesians 2:8-10. What do these verses say about why we are here and what we are to do?

Galatians 1:10 reveals something wonderful about the character of Paul. Read this verse and discuss the pressures in our society and the "Hamans" we could potentially bow down to or try to please. What do Paul and Mordecai have in common?

Read Daniel 4:34-35. Nebuchadnezzar was another king with unreasonable and erratic behavior. What happened to him and how was his attitude changed?

What stories of Israel's past encounters with Yahweh do you think brought Esther comfort during her days in the palace of Xerxes? Did she remind herself of all Mordecai taught her about His character and faithfulness? What do you think?

King Xerxes was not accessible to his people. He was shielded from bad news or interruptions. Only a select few could approach him and only at certain times. Contrast his style of leadership with what we learn of our King Jesus in Hebrews 4:14-16.

How does Joseph's statement in Genesis 50:20 compare to Esther 4:14?

When Esther said, "If I perish, I perish" the odds were against her. The law of the land said that no one could interrupt the king. The government said that she and all Jews should die. And being a woman, the society she lived in viewed her as a sex object. Also, the man closest to the king was intent on destroying everything that mattered to her. Have you ever felt the circumstances of your life were against you? Have you ever been under the authority of an unreasonable person? What was it like? How did you handle the situation? What can you do? What would God have you believe?

The old phrase "what goes around comes around" certainly applies to Haman. How can Numbers 32:23 comfort us as well as convict us?

There's an old saying that goes, "Pride is the only known disease that makes everybody sick except the person who has it." Contrast Haman's ego trip with Proverbs 16:18.

Galatians 4:4 begins, "When the fullness of time was come… ." Discuss God's timing in the release of Joseph from prison, the honoring of Mordecai for saving the king's life, and the birth of Jesus.

Haman got up on his last day on earth excited about seeing Mordecai's body impaled on his gallows. Instead, he spent the day leading a parade to honor Mordecai in the streets of Susa. If Haman had been of a humbler nature, he might have seen this as an opportunity to repent. Read Psalm 33:10-11, Proverbs 21:30, and Romans 8:31. Make a practical application of these verses to your life situation.

If you could have a conversation with Esther, what stories of your own would you share with her about circumstances in your life that have felt out of control and hopeless? What victories in your walk with Jesus would you share with her?

Share stories of the sovereignty of God in your life. Looking back, were you aware of his hand in the events of your life?

The story we have of Esther shows us one dramatic moment in which she stepped forward in a very public way and was obedient to God. She received national recognition for her actions in an empire of 100 million people. Most of us will never be called on to do something like that. We find ourselves stepping forward in other ways, most of them quiet and unseen. Discuss ways we are called to be an Esther today.

Discuss the way Esther prepared before she stood before the king. How can we prepare before facing each challenge in life? What is available to us?

Mordecai was honored for saving Xerxes' life five years after the fact. Have you ever felt overlooked or underappreciated? What can we learn from Mordecai?

How can we as Christians have an "orphan mentality?" What is the truth about our place in God's family and our position in Christ?

Esther was around thirty years old when Xerxes was assassinated. What do you imagine her life was like when she was no longer queen?

What does Esther teach us about trusting the timing of God?

WEEK TWELVE DISCUSSION QUESTIONS: Deborah

Deborah was a woman used to sitting under a date tree and settling disputes among the Israelites. Then suddenly her circumstances change drastically. She goes from the date tree to the front lines of battle and operates with grace and courage. Why was she able to do this?

Discuss ways that women today can be ready, with the calm assurance of the Holy Spirit's sufficiency in us, to meet every crisis when it comes.

How we behave in times of crisis shows what we really believe. How do we prepare for those times? What kind of foundation must be in place?

Deborah was proactive. She knew God had called her to do something, and she went forward to fulfill it. What is the difference between walking in a place of leadership and merely taking charge of a situation?

Judges 5 shows us a victory song Deborah sang over her people. In it she recounts the powerful deliverance of God. In Zephaniah 3:17, we see that God sings over us as well. In light of your present circumstances, what do you think God is singing over you? Remember, his heart is for you to be encouraged.

We live in a society where people believe there is no absolute truth. How do we relate to people and share the gospel with those who believe that all paths lead to God? What risks do we take proclaiming our faith in Jesus alone as the way, the truth and the life?

When Deborah saw spiritual revival take place in the Israelites, she rejoiced. Her focus was not on herself. She cared nothing about getting the glory at the end of the battle. She was thrilled to see the change of heart in her people. Take some time to think about what motivates your actions. Discuss ways we can tell if our egos are in control. How do we react when no one gives us the credit we feel we deserve?

King Jabin was raised up by God to discipline the Israelites. Has God ever used anyone in your life to discipline you? What was it like?

When the Israelites cried out to God in the midst of their suffering, they were asking for relief instead of forgiveness. Compare this attitude with David's prayer in Psalm 51:10. What kind of attitude would God be most pleased to see in us?

Barak hesitated when God told him what to do. So did Moses and Gideon when God commissioned them as well. All these men are listed in the Hebrews Hall of Faith. What does this tell us about the patience of God? What does this tell us about the kind of people God can use to accomplish his purposes?

When God told Barak to go into battle, Israel had very few weapons at the time and no prepared army. God knew what he was about to do for his people, but they didn't. How was this a test? How does God test us today?

Sisera's army had 900 iron chariots. What odds are you facing in your present circumstances that seem to ensure your defeat?

God not only sent a violent rainstorm and a flooding river to defeat Sisera. He also confused the enemy troops and threw them into a panic. When God fights for you, your enemy is routed. In what ways do you need God to fight for you? What kind of faith does this require of you?

Jael had previously been living in a neutral condition between Israel and the Canaanites. She and her family were friendly with both sides. When she took the tent peg in her hand, she went from being neutral to clearly taking her stand with the God of Israel. Discuss areas in our lives where we need to go from neutral to a clear stand on the side of godliness.

What do you think of the fact that Deborah referred to herself as a mother of Israel? What was her job description? How does this elevate motherhood in your thinking?

What would Deborah have to say about the women's lib movement? What does it mean to be comfortable with your identity? What is your identity based on?

How would you describe the times that Deborah lived in? According to Judges 4:1-3 and Judges 5:6-8, the people believed there was no absolute truth. Can you relate?

Deborah had a way of judging that kept men from feeling threatened. What can we learn from her?

Joshua 1:2-9 is God's ideal for his children. How does God want us to "possess the land?"

What has been "left in your land" to test you and teach you? What favorite verses encourage you in your battles? "Greater is he that is…."

Read Psalm 83:9-10. What was said of Barak's victory? As women, what kind of power do we have with our words? Why do you think Barak wanted her to go with him? (See Exodus 33:14-15.)

Deborah believed for revival for her people in really bad times. What does this say to us?

Discuss the C. S. Lewis quote, "Crisis is an atmosphere for miracles."

Judges 4:14 says, "The Lord has gone out before you." Psalm 23 says, "He has prepared a table before me in the presence of my enemies." There is no place the shepherd of your soul will lead you where he has not already gone before you! What does this mean for your present circumstances?

How does this story inspire you to pray for your leaders at church? In government? In your workplace?

Have a little fun. Discuss practical choices you can make today that can change your world and bring glory to Jesus.

ENDNOTES

Week Two

1   Terry C. Muck (editor), *Faith in Action Study Bible: Living God's World in a Changing World (New International Version)*, Zondervan, Grand Rapids, MI, 2005, page 990.

2   National Right to Life, www. nrlc. org.

3   Earl D. Radmacher, Ronald B. Allen, and H.W. House, *Nelson's New Illustrated Bible Com   mentary: Spreading the Light of God's Word into Your Life*, Thomas Nelson, Nashville, TN, 1999, page 751.

4   *Nelson's New Illustrated Bible Commentary*, page 89.

Week Four

5   Earl D. Radmacher, Ronald B. Allen, and H.W. House, *Nelson's New Illustrated Bible Commentary: Spreading the Light of God's Word into Your Life*, Thomas Nelson, Nashville, TN, 1999, page 89.

Week Five

6   Bryant G. Wood, "Did the Israelites Conquer Jericho?" *Biblical Archaeology Review*, Vol. 16, Issue 2, March-April 1990, page 44-58.

7   Ernst Sellin and Carl Watzinger, *Jericho die Ergebnisse der Ausgrabungen*, Otto Zeller Verlag, Osnabruck, 1973 (reprint of 1913 edition), page 58.

8   Earl D. Radmacher, Ronald B. Allen, and H.W. House, *Nelson's New Illustrated Bible Commentary: Spreading the Light of God's Word into Your Life*, Thomas Nelson, Nashville, TN, 1999, page 275.

9   "Jericho," WebBible Encyclopedia, http://www. christiananswers. net, accessed 6 May 2009.

Week Six

10 Terry C. Muck (editor), *Faith in Action Study Bible: Living God's World in a Changing World (New International Version)*, Zondervan, Grand Rapids, MI, 2005, page 62.

11 Earl D. Radmacher, Ronald B. Allen, and H.W. House, *Nelson's New Illustrated Bible Commentary: Spreading the Light of God's Word into Your Life*, Thomas Nelson, Nashville, TN, 1999, page 67.

12 *Nelson's New Illustrated Bible Commentary*, page 68.

13 Ibid.

Week Seven

14 Bonnie Keen, *Blessed Are the Desperate*, Harvest House/Julie Rose Music, Eugene, OR, 2000, page 92.

15 RAINN/Rape, Abuse & Incest National Network,   http://www. rainn. org, accessed July, 2009.

16 Susan Forward, Ph. D. , "Innocence and Betrayal Overcoming the Legacy of Sexual Abuse," Wisconsin Coalition   Against Sexual Assault, http://www. wcasa. org, accessed 2004.

17 Susan Forward, Ph. D. , "Memory," Wisconsin Coalition Against Sexual Assault, http://www. wcasa. org, accessed 2004.

18 "National Crime Victimization Survey," Bureau of Justice, 2000.

Week Eight:

19 Earl D. Radmacher, Ronald B. Allen, and H.W. House, *Nelson's New Illustrated Bible Commentary: Spreading the Light of God's Word into Your Life*, Thomas Nelson, Nashville, TN, 1999, page 53.

20 H. Clay Trumbull, *Studies in Oriental Social Life*, John D. Wattles & Co. , Philadelphia, PA, 1894, page 11.

21 Hilma N. Granqvist, *Marriage Conditions in a Palestinian Village*, AMS Press & Co. , New York, 1931, page 13.

22 Dayspring Calendar.

23 Frederick Buechner, *The Son of Laughter*, Harper, San Francisco, CA, 993, pages 111-112.

24 Warren W. Wiersbe, *Wiersbe Bible Commentary*. P. 105, David C. Cook, 2007, Colorado Springs, CO

25 *Marriage Conditions in a Palestinian Village*, pages 44-45.

26 *The Son of Laughter*, pages 112-115.

27 *The Son of Laughter*, page 115.

28 *Nelson's New Illustrated Bible Commentary*, page 54.

29 Philip Yancey, *Disappointment with God*, Zondervan, Grand Rapids, MI, 1988, page 71.

30 "The Solid Rock", text: Edward Mote, music: William B. Bradbury, copyright 1997 by Integrity's Hosanna Music and Word Music, Nashville, TN

Week Nine

31 Earl D. Radmacher, Ronald B. Allen, and H.W. House, *Nelson's New Illustrated Bible Commentary: Spreading the Light of God's Word into Your Life*, Thomas Nelson, Nashville, TN, 1999, page 53.

32 Internet, Jewish Wedding Customs and Their Origins, www. laydownlife. net/yedidah/ ancientJewishweddingceremony.

33 C.S. Lewis, *Mere Christianity*, Macmillan Publishing, London, England, 1952, page 163.

34 Frederick Buechner, *The Son of Laughter*, Harper, San Francisco, 1993, pages 120-121.

35 *Nelson's New Illustrated Bible Commentary, page 738*

36 Bonnie Keen and David Hamilton, "My Beloved," *God of Many Chances*, Julie Rose Music, Inc., Word Publishing, ASCAP, 2004.

Week Ten

37 Earl D. Radmacher, Ronald B. Allen, and H.W. House, *Nelson's New Illustrated Bible Commentary: Spreading the Light of God's Word into Your Life*, Thomas Nelson, Nashville, TN, 1999, page 606.

38 Ibid.

Week Eleven

39 Charles Swindoll, *Esther*, Thomas Nelson, Nashville, TN, 1997, page 120.

40 *Esther*, pages 180-181.

41 Arthur Bennett (editor), "Covenant," *The Valley of Vision*, Banner of Truth Trust, Carlisle, PA, page 259.

Week Twelve

42 Earl D. Radmacher, Ronald B. Allen, and H.W. House, *Nelson's New Illustrated Bible Commentary: Spreading the Light of God's Word into Your Life*, Thomas Nelson, Nashville, TN, 1999, page 312.

43 *NIV Study Bible, 2002, Zondervan Publishing, Grand Rapids, MI*

44 Scotty Smith, *Living By Faith in An Unbelieving World: A Study of Ezekiel, Daniel and the Life of Joseph*, Christ Community Church, Nashville, TN, 2005. Week 4, pages 5-6.

45 *NIV Study Bible, 2002, Zondervan Publishing, Grand Rapids, MI*

46 Emil G. Hirsch and Gerson B. Levi, "Palm," *Jewish Encyclopedia,* Scotty Smith, *Living By Faith in An Unbelieving World: A Study of Ezekiel, Daniel and the Life of Joseph,* Christ Community Church, Nashville, TN, 2005. Week 4, pages 5-6.

47 *Living By Faith in An Unbelieving World,* Scotty Smith, *Living By Faith in An Unbelieving World: A Study of Ezekiel, Daniel and the Life of Joseph,* Christ Community Church, Nashville, TN, 2005. Week 4, pages 5-6.

48 Ibid.

HOW TO ORDER

If you have enjoyed WOMEN WHO DARE TO BELIEVE Volume One and would like to continue this series, we invite you to begin Volume Two. While the first study explored the lives of biblical heroines from the Old Testament, Part Two focuses mainly on women in the New Testament. Come with us as we get to know Anna, the woman with the issue of blood, Mary the mother of Jesus, and many others. These women of the Way will encourage you in your own walk and will come to life for you as never before.

If you would like to order copies of WOMEN WHO DARE TO BELIEVE Volume Two, or receive information about the accompanying musical by the same name, please contact us at www.christianmusicalsforwomen.com.

LaVergne, TN USA
24 September 2010
198222LV00002B/8/P